CONT...
with the
AMERICAN FAMILY

CONTRACT
with the
AMERICAN FAMILY

A bold plan by
Christian Coalition to
strengthen the family and restore
common-sense values

INTRODUCTION BY
RALPH REED
Executive Director, Christian Coalition

MOORINGS
Nashville, Tennesee
A Division of The Ballantine Publishing Group, Random House, Inc.

CONTRACT WITH THE AMERICAN FAMILY

Contents

Acknowledgments

As with any project, there are more people to thank than space or time permit. Contract with the American Family was a corporate effort by a group of very talented people.

None more so than those on Christian Coalition staff. Heidi Scanlon and Marshall Wittmann of our governmental affairs office made the Contract their final work before departing. Susan Muskett supervised the project, turning disparate ideas into a cohesive and compelling document. Mike Russell helped get the message out and worked with the media. And Brian Lopina, our new Director of Governmental Affairs, helped make this his first Christian Coalition effort.

They were all assisted by so many people in the pro-family movement: Phyllis Schlafly at Eagle Forum, Douglas Johnson at National Right to Life, Colleen Parro at RNC for Life, Pat Trueman at American Family Association, and others too numerous to mention.

But the thanks don't end there. For the ideas that became the Contract later mushroomed into this book. This enormous effort was made possible by the hard, thoughtful, and timely work of Douglas Johnson, Rich Lowry, Eric Berger, Susan Muskett, and Jeff Peck. To all of them many, many thanks. And finally, thanks to David Kuo, who brought it together and turned it out.

Introduction
by Ralph Reed, Jr.
Executive Director, Christian Coalition

ON MAY 17, 1995 CHRISTIAN COALITION held a press conference to announce the ten points in the *Contract with the American Family*. In a room in the U.S. Capitol, we were joined by forty of our fifty state affiliates and by other concerned citizens. In addition, we were joined by a number of prominent senators and congressmen including Speaker of the House of Representatives Newt Gingrich.

The presence of so many people was both important and symbolic. Important because it represented an historic day in American politics—a day where pro-family policies took center stage and were finally given the attention they deserve. It was symbolic because the *Contract with the American Family* is a document full of ideas that came from the grass roots.

While the media has frequently caricatured people of faith active in the political process as "fire-breathing radicals" or "poor, uneducated, and easy to command," the reality is very different. People of faith in this country want for their families, for their communities, and for their country what almost everyone else wants. We want a nation of safe neighborhoods, strong families, limited government, lower taxes, term limits, and schools that work.

We believe in an America where all citizens are judged on the content of their character, and not their gender, race, religion, or ethnic background. We believe in an America where parents can send children to the schools of their choice—the best schools for their children, whether they be public, private, or parochial. We envision a nation where parents can be fully confident that their children are learning how to read and how to write, that they are safe, and that they are going to be able to master the disciplines of math and science and history and geography, far beyond the level of their counterparts around the world.

They want an America where their children can walk to a playground three blocks from home and not worry whether they are going to come back alive. An America where more marriages succeed than fail, where more children are born in wedlock than outside of it, and where children are counted both by families and by government as a blessing rather than a burden.

I have long said that that is our agenda and our desire. Following the November elections—when conservatives took control of the Senate and House—we were bombarded with questions like: "Now that you and Christian Coalition have gained a place at the table, what will you seek to legislate? What will be your agenda, not only for yourselves, but for the nation?" For religious conservatives, who have finally gained a voice in the conversation that we call democracy, those are important and relevant questions.

We began to answer those questions early this year when Christian Coalition launched one of the largest grass-roots campaigns in our nation's history. We worked on behalf of the balanced budget amendment, family tax relief, welfare reform, and term limits. We supported the

Contract with America not only because it dealt with economic issues, but because we felt that it dealt with many important cultural issues such as crime, pornography, and adoption.

Christian Coalition answers another part of those questions with the release of the *Contract with the American Family*, which contains ten proposals that will hold government accountable for the cultural crisis that has afflicted our nation over the past three decades. *The Contract with the American Family* is, we believe, a bold and a dramatic agenda to strengthen families and restore commonsense values.

This is not a Christian agenda. It is not a Republican agenda. It is not a special interest agenda. It is a pro-family agenda, and it is supported by the vast majority of the American people, Republican and Democrat, Christian and Jew, black and white, Protestant and Catholic.

These provisions are the ten suggestions, not the Ten Commandments. The *Contract with the American Family* is a public policy document, not a theological statement. It is designed to help Congress as it charts a cultural agenda after the first hundred days.

Our purpose is to present a blueprint on how to address what we believe are the most pressing issues in American politics today: the fraying of the social fabric, the coarsening of the culture, the breakdown of the family, and a decline in civility. We have no intention of doing to this Congress what the unions, the feminists, and the gay lobby did to President Clinton when he took office two-and-a-half years ago. They presented an extremist agenda and forced this administration out of the mainstream on many issues. The Clinton administration stumbled out of the starting gate, and it never fully recovered.

Our approach has been very different. We have been patient, willing to listen, and ready to engage in a mutually constructive dialogue. And as we unveil a cultural agenda for this Congress, we present a mainstream and reasonable approach, one that is stated with respect for our foes as well as our friends and which enjoys the support of a majority of the American people.

Why do we do this? We do this for one very simple reason: Even if Congress balances the budget and lowers taxes, yet we still live in a nation in which our inner cities resemble Beirut, in which our children pass through metal detectors into schools that are war zones, and one out of every three children is born out of wedlock, we will have failed as a society.

Our goal is not to legislate family values, it is to ensure that Washington values families.

The *Contract with the American Family* includes a religious equality amendment which will guarantee every American's right to religious faith and its expression. It contains vitally needed proposals for promoting school choice, returning control of education to the local level, passing a mother's and homemaker's rights act to give tax equity to women who work in the home and want to save for their retirement, privatizing the arts, and protecting innocent human life.

It is important for all of those involved in politics to remember that a political agenda is just that: a *political* agenda. Such an agenda seeks to pass laws to protect those things that need to be protected. It seeks to right wrongs. But it is, finally, a political and legislative agenda with limited impact. Certainly, it can make a change in our society, but it cannot create the kind of society in which we all want to live.

Nevertheless, the *Contract with the American Family* represents a valuable contribution to a congressional agenda beyond the first hundred days. There is no deadline or specified time period during which these items are to be enacted. But Congress would be well advised to act with all due and deliberate speed. The provisions in the contract enjoy support from 60 to 90 percent of the American people.

These items do not represent the pro-family movement's entire agenda. There are many other prominent and outstanding pro-family organizations who are going to be making their own contributions. We look forward to working with them. This contract is designed to be the first word, not the last, in developing a bold and incremental start to strengthening the family and restoring values.

1

Restoring Religious Equality

A constitutional amendment to protect the religious liberties of Americans in public places.

WITH EACH PASSING YEAR, people of faith grow increasingly distressed by the hostility of public institutions toward religious expression. We have witnessed the steady erosion of the time-honored rights of religious Americans—both as individuals and as communities—to practice what they believe in the public square. This erosion has been abetted by a court system which stands the plain meaning of the First Amendment on its head. The time has now come to amend the Constitution to restore freedom of speech for America's people of faith.

Under the Religious Equality Amendment, all citizens, including students, would be free to express their faith in noncompulsory settings and in ways that affirm their convictions without infringing upon the rights of others.

This balanced, common-sense approach would not mean a return to the days of organized, sectarian prayer in public schools. But it would mean a 180-degree turn from an America where, today, courts suppress free speech in the name of upholding it.

Censoring Religious Expression

Examples of hostility toward religious values and those who hold them abound. In Nevada, an elementary school student chosen to sing a solo in the school's Christmas pageant was forbidden from singing "The First Noel" because of its religious overtones.[1] At a public elementary school in Rhode Island, the principal announced shortly before the beginning of a Christmas concert that he had censored all of the pageant's songs.[2] A Scarsdale, New York, school board banned all religious celebrations from schools, although parties with nonholiday themes were still permitted. According to the Catholic League for Religious and Civil Rights, the ban included "displays or exhibits, such as wreaths, garlands, caroling, and menorahs that appear to promote or give approval to religious matters," as well as "candy canes, bells, holiday music, and Hanukkah or Christmas parties and concerts."[3] Teachers in New Jersey were told to avoid references to Easter, including jelly beans and the colors purple and yellow.

Children have been told they cannot read the Bible during silent reading time.[4] In one school, a little girl was told there was a problem with the book she chose to read to her class—it mentioned "God" four times.[5]

This antireligious bigotry is not confined to the classroom. The Supreme Court has seen to it that nativity scenes are now barred from federal post offices[6] and from the lawns of public buildings unless accompanied by a nonreligious display such as Santa Claus. Some courthouses are prohibited from displaying the Ten Commandments (despite the fact that they are chiseled into the walls of the United States Supreme Court). And landlords have been sued by the state for discrimination because they refused to rent to unmarried couples for religious reasons.[7]

The founders of our nation knew that America was, first and foremost, a haven of religious liberty. Among the rights enumerated in the First Amendment, religious liberty was the cornerstone: "Congress shall make no law respecting an establishment of religion, or prohibiting the free exercise therefore. . . ."

Protecting People of Faith

This amendment to the Bill of Rights was intended to protect the churches from government encroachment, and not the other way around. A quick perusal of the case law and the legislative and Constitutional arguments confronted by the Founding Fathers reveals that they were very concerned about hurting the church. Initial drafts of the First Amendment showed their intent. On June 8, 1789, James Madison brought this proposal: "The civil rights of none shall be abridged on account of religious belief or worship, nor shall any national religion be established, nor shall the full and equal rights of conscience be in any manner, or on any pretext, infringed." The House Select Committee offered this on August 15: "No religion shall be established by law, nor shall the equal rights of conscience be infringed." After a day of debate it was modified to read, "Congress shall make no laws touching religion, or infringing the rights of conscience." Finally, "Congress shall make no law establishing religion, or to prevent the free exercise thereof, or to infringe the rights of conscience." That draft was subsequently sent to the Senate which came up with its own language. Both were reconciled in a conference committee.

The First Amendment, far from unique, was actually a reflection of language that existed in state constitutions. For instance, part 1, article 2 of the Massachusetts constitution in 1780 read, "It is the right, as well as the duty, of all men in society, publicly, and at stated seasons, to worship the Supreme Being, the Great Creator and Preserver of the universe. . . ." South Carolina's constitution of 1778 reflected the same sentiment. Article 38 stated, "That all persons and religious societies who acknowledge that there is one God, and a future state of rewards and punishments, and that God is publicly worshipped, shall be freely tolerated. . . . That all denominations of Christians . . . in this State, demeaning themselves peaceably and faithfully, shall enjoy equal religious and civil privileges."

Such freedom, however, is no longer a given. That is why Christian Coalition supports a Religious Equality Amendment. Such an amendment would ensure that all citizens, including students, would be free to express their faith in noncompulsory settings and in ways that affirm their convictions without infringing on the rights of others.

But how have the courts managed to use the First Amendment itself to subvert fundamental religious freedoms? It has happened through their misinterpretation of the first ten words of the First Amendment, the so-called "establishment clause." The Founding Fathers intended the establishment clause to ensure that America's political institutions would never be used to benefit one religion at

4

the expense of another, and that America's churches would not involve themselves in purely political disputes. They believed that the European system of officially sanctioned "state religions" benefited neither the state nor the religion involved. Indeed, it was from such systems that the Pilgrims and Puritans fled. This is what is rightly meant by the phrase *separation of church and state.*

Guaranteeing Religious Vitality

It is interesting to note that the very term *separation of church and state* originated not in any law, but in a speech by Baptist preacher Roger Williams, who said, "When they have opened a gap in the hedge or wall of separation between the garden of the church and the wilderness of the world, God hath ever broke down the wall itself. . . . And that there fore if He will eer please to restore His garden and paradise again, it must of necessity be walled in peculiarly unto Himself and the world."[8] Following this, in a letter to the Danbury Baptists on January 1, 1802, Jefferson wrote, "I contemplate [in] solemn reverence that act of the whole American people which declared that their legislature should 'make no law respecting an establishment of religion, or prohibiting the free exercise thereof,' thus building a wall of separation between Church and State." As the Founding Fathers recognized, this concept is an essential underpinning of a democratic society and the best guarantee of a nation's religious vitality.

Since the early 1960s, however, the courts in general—and the Supreme Court in particular—have taken a radically different view of the First Amendment. Over time, the courts began to see the establishment clause not as a guarantee of, but as a counterweight to, the right to religious "free exercise." Radical left groups such as the American Civil Liberties Union urged with increasing success that religion itself be viewed not as a positive influence, but as something suspect, perhaps inherently coercive, often incompatible with practical democracy and the rights of minorities.

In the eyes of many judges, separation of church and state was no longer a means of protecting religious practice from government oppression. It became a mandate to the government to root out religious expression from all areas of public life—and especially from public schools. The establishment clause was transformed from a shield for religion into a cover for the official sanctioning of religious intolerance.

Eliminating Public Expressions of Faith

In 1962, the Supreme Court banned organized prayer from public schools. Since then, federal, state, and local courts and officials, including public school administrators, have joined in a nationwide search and destroy mission for student religious practices. For example, a St. Louis fourth-grader was recently given three days' detention for bowing his head and whispering a quick grace over his cafeteria lunch. In school districts across the country, high school seniors are forbidden to mention "God," "Jesus Christ," or similar words in their graduation speeches. Cheerleaders have been barred from praying at after-hours pep rallies in Texas. Christian student groups are routinely denied the use of school facilities and forbidden to meet on school grounds. Children are forbidden to use Bibles in show and tell, and in some cases to bring Bibles into classrooms at all. Students have gotten in on the act, too. A poster-sized print of a famous painting of Jesus donated to a Michigan school in the 1930s was removed after a senior sued during his senior year, claiming the picture proved school administrators were promoting religion. Never mind the fact that the subject was not only a prominent historical figure, but perhaps the most famous teacher of all time.

Establishment clause cases are not restricted to public buildings or public lands. State governments have sued property owners for, among other things, refusing on religious grounds to rent rooms to unmarried couples. At a time when their relief efforts are sorely needed, private charities across the country have been hamstrung by laws limiting federal grants and aid to organizations that have stripped their programs of all religious content.

Despite the number and scope of these examples, our legal culture's hostility to faith has not gone smoothly. Partly because of their contradictory interpretation of the First Amendment, courts have never decided exactly how to determine when God has trespassed on the public domain. Courts today are still bound by the 1971 case of *Lemon v. Kurtzman*, in which the U.S. Supreme Court attempted to draft rules to clarify when government action violates the establishment clause.

According to the "*Lemon* test," the government may not perform any act that (1) does not have a "secular legislative purpose," (2) either "advances" or "inhibits" religion, or (3) leads to "an excessive government entanglement with religion." Unfortunately, Supreme Court decisions which have since attempted to apply the "*Lemon* test" have not only failed to clarify any of these rules; they

7

have muddied the legal waters to such a degree that local, state, and federal officials are unclear—and often at odds —as to what kinds of religious expression are to be protected or denied.

For example, since *Lemon:*

• The Supreme Court has held in one case that the government can pay for buses to take students to and from religious schools, but in another case that the government cannot pay for buses to take such students on educational field trips.[9]

• Parochial school students have been allowed in one ruling to borrow textbooks from the government, but forbidden in another to borrow other state-owned "instructional materials" such as lab equipment, movies, or maps.

• While the Court struck down a New York program of partial tuition tax credits for parents with children in nonpublic schools (including religious schools), it upheld a Minnesota plan to allow the parents of nonprofit school students to take tax deductions not only for tuition, but for transportation and "nonreligious" textbooks too.

So the *Lemon* test, in practice, turns out not to be a test at all, but a way for courts (particularly the Supreme Court) to cloak contradictory outcomes in seemingly objective terms. While the Supreme Court has distanced itself from *Lemon* in recent years, no five justices can agree on a standard to replace it. So *Lemon* remains the law of the land—and people of faith find their free speech rights trapped in a legal limbo.

Protecting Free Speech for Religion

In the meantime, hostility to religious expression continues to find outlets in lawsuits across the land. Each new lawsuit seeks to expand the size of the "religion-free zone" in the public square—and to expand the definition of "public square" to envelop more of the lives of individuals and their communities. Given the course of events since 1962, what can we expect as the next development in First Amendment jurisprudence?

Certain groups are already actively seeking to expel chaplains from the armed forces and the U.S. Senate, to stop the practice of opening sessions of Congress with prayer, and to eliminate references to God in government buildings and public documents—including our currency.

It is time for people of faith in America to restore the right to freedom of religious expression. It is time to reilluminate the meaning of the First Amendment and the fundamental liberties it offers to all of citizens. It is time to reclaim for religious expression the free speech protections it never should have lost.

Some may argue that extending First Amendment rights to such religious expression as voluntary, student-initiated prayer by a high school valedictorian at a graduation ceremony is somehow "coercive." But if attendance at a graduation ceremony is voluntary, how can one student be "coerced" into participating in a prayer offered by another? Simply hearing others pray may be unpleasant for some students, but isn't that the price of freedom of speech? No student would be able to sue on Constitutional grounds if the valedictorian elaborated political

9

views with which he or she disagreed. Should religious speech be accorded less protection than political speech?

Furthermore, is it not part of the mission of a public school to promote tolerance, respect for the values of others and appreciation of diversity? If so, allowing students freely to discuss their opinions on their deepest convictions will only further these goals.

Others may object that a Religious Equality Amendment will simply establish a state religion by the back door. It will have the opposite effect. By forcing the government to expel all religious expression from the public sphere, the current judicial interpretation has marginalized faith in our public life. A Religious Equality Amendment will simply restore the free-speech rights of religious Americans to equality with those already enjoyed by their nonreligious fellow citizens.

Still others may agree with the concept of a Religious Equality Amendment but hesitate to endorse changing the Constitution. But the Constitution itself provides the amendment mechanism to allow the will of the people to assert itself where, as now, fundamental rights are being flouted and the courts have neither the will nor the wisdom to enforce the spirit of our national charter. Also, a Religious Equality Amendment would not represent an attempt to add some new right to the Constitution, but to revitalize the right at the very heart of the First Amendment.

Since the Supreme Court struck down school prayer in 1962, Americans have, in annual polls, supported school prayer by margins of 70 to 80 percent. A Luntz Research Company poll shows support for a Religious Equality Amendment at 78 percent of all Americans.[10] And in a

10

country where public school students are not allowed to hear about God in the classroom, 96 percent of Americans believe that he exists.

Of course, these numbers do not, by themselves, demonstrate that passing a Religious Equality Amendment would be right. But they do support the fact that America has remained, as it was founded, a nation of citizens who hold religious faith and practice in high regard. These numbers confirm that Americans do not believe that religious expression is unworthy of the protection our constitution is supposed to extend to all speech. They clearly illustrate the "disconnect" between America's people of faith and the political and legal culture. And they show that, someday soon, a Religious Equality Amendment to the Constitution or a statute may be a reality.

2

Local Control of Education

Transfer funding of the federal Department of Education to families and local school boards.

EVERY CHILD IN AMERICA has the right to expect three things from our educational system: a safe learning environment, a school that teaches basic skills, and instruction that reinforces rather than undermines traditional values. Sadly, the public schools loaded down with mandates and directives from a Washington bureaucracy are failing to deliver these essentials of education to our children. Parents are distressed over the failure of schools to teach children values and the basic skills of reading, writing, and arithmetic.

The Department of Education was established at the end of the Carter Administration, just in time to preside over the continued precipitous decline of American education. Since the 1960s, SAT scores have dropped by more than seventy-five points.[1] To ease the embarrassment, the College Board has resorted to a dumbed-down scoring system so test-takers can miss questions and still get a "perfect" score. Ten nations outperform American thirteen-year-olds in math and science tests.[2]

Increasingly, it is not learning that goes on in American schools, but something scarier and more dangerous. Metal detectors routinely greet students at school doors in the morning. There are 250,000 crimes committed on school property each year. In 1992, 10 percent of tenth-graders said they had taken a weapon to school in the past month. Americans desperately need to get control of their schools.

One of the most important imperatives is to ensure that schools reinforce values taught in the home.

Too often, sex education emphasizes contraception and condom use rather than abstinence and self-control. Homosexuality is promoted as an acceptable alternative lifestyle. The newest educational philosophy, outcome-based education (OBE), supplants teaching of basic skills. Psychological counseling takes place without parental involvement or notification.[3]

For fifteen years, the department has only worsened the nation's educational crisis. It is time to admit that in the most important test facing it, the one on which the future of a generation of American young people depends, the Department of Education has flunked.

President Carter sought a Department of Education in the first place as a way to appease the largest teachers union, the National Education Association (NEA). The NEA endorsed Carter in the 1976 presidential election—its first-ever endorsement of a candidate—because of his commitment to create the department, which the union envisioned as a way to further its interests in Washington, D.C. From its inception, the department has functioned as a tool of the education establishment, a force for the status quo rather than for change, a friend of the bureaucrats and "experts" rather than ordinary parents.

As one writer for *The Chronicle of Education* reported, the NEA "has attacked parents' moves to gain more control, saying that they have gone overboard and that teachers cannot be effective under parental control." Meanwhile, the NEA has supported gay rights, a nuclear freeze, teacher strikes, and school-based clinics that dispense condoms. This attitude—that parents had best butt out and let the "enlightened" and "sophisticated" ones educate their children—has permeated much of the department's work.

Control of Education Shifts to Washington, D.C.

When it was created, the department had a budget of approximately $15 billion and some 140 separate programs. Even then, responsible questions were raised about the influence it would have on American education. Representative John Erlenborn, a Republican from Illinois, wrote at the time, that there would be "interference in textbook choices, curricula, staffing, salaries, the make-up of student bodies, building designs, and all other irritants that the government has invented to harass the population. These decisions which are now made in the local school or school district will slowly but surely be transferred to Washington." Prescient words, but Erlenborn wasn't the only one to voice concern. Stanford University president Richard W. Lyman testified before Congress that "the two-hundred-year-old absence of a Department of Education is not the result of simple failure during all that time. On the contrary, it derives from the conviction that we do not want the kinds of educational systems that such arrangements produce." Since then the department's budget has doubled, adding about one hundred more programs, and it has steadily, seemingly inexorably, shifted control of American education from where it belongs—in the hands of parents and local communities—to Washington, D.C.

Model Standards Established

The most recent attempts to grasp power came in 1993 and 1994 with the passage of the "Goals 2000" program and the re-authorization of the *Elementary and Secondary Education Act* (ESEA), also known as the "Improving America's Schools Act." Goals 2000 is an extraordinary usurpation of the American tradition of local control of education. Despite a ban on the Department of Education interfering in curricular decisions, Goals 2000 establishes "model standards" for curriculum and creates a kind of national school board, the National Education Standards and Improvement Council, to certify these standards and others for student performance. The standards are not technically binding on states, but Goals 2000 gives them national standing and requires that states "voluntarily" develop comparable standards to receive the billions of dollars in funding that the federal government doles out. This amounts to a sort of implicit federal blackmail. *ESEA* continued the trend, tightening federal controls and imposing new ones on states and localities. It even imposes a version of outcome based education on school systems for their disadvantaged children.

There is perhaps no better proof of the danger of federal involvement in education than the recently released model national history standards. Developed with $2.2

million in federal funding from the National Endowment for the Humanities and the Department of Education, they are a monument to what is wrong with an education establishment that is out of touch with the values of ordinary Americans. In the thirty-one standards for U.S. history, for example, the U.S. Constitution was not mentioned once but instead it was relegated to the supporting materials.[4]

The establishment of the National Organization of Women and Sierra Club were regarded as notable events in the standards, but not the first convening of the U.S. Congress.[5] Thomas Edison, Robert E. Lee, the Wright Brothers, and Albert Einstein got no mention at all. According to one reviewer, the material had only one quotation from a congressional leader: former House Speaker Tip O'Neill calling Ronald Reagan "a cheerleader for selfishness."[6] The world history standards were also controversial for their anti-Western bias.[7] The Senate voted ninety-nine to one to condemn them.

American Students Behind on Math and Science

American education must change. Nearly every report on education tells the same story. In 1989 an international comparison showed American students scoring at the bottom of mathematics and science skills while the South Koreans scored at the top. But that's not all. When asked if they were good at math, 68 percent of Americans said yes, the highest percentage for any country. Only 23 percent of South Koreans thought they were good, the lowest. The 1991 National Assessment of Educational Progress found 72 percent of fourth-graders can do third grade math, only 14 percent of eighth-graders can do seventh-grade math, and only 5 percent of high school seniors display the skills necessary to do college-level math. Studies have shown that more than two-thirds of high school seniors did not know the half-century in which the Civil War took place and less than a quarter were able to say within twenty years when Abraham Lincoln was president.

The solution to disturbing figures such as these is not more spending on education, especially at the federal level. In fact, federal spending has boomed while American education has declined. Before the explosion of federal spending with the arrival of the Great Society in the mid-sixties, federal spending on elementary and secondary education amounted to less than $1 billion. Most of it went to vocational schools in a long-standing federal program. But by 1995 federal spending had skyrocketed to $16 billion. And what is there to show for it? The chief federal program is called Chapter One. Meant to give extra federal dollars to districts with high proportions of "educationally disadvantaged" children, the $7 billion program in fact sends money indiscriminately to districts all across the nation. In its 1995 budget the Clinton Administration summed up the nation's experience with Chapter One this way: "National evaluation studies by independent groups and the Department of Education document that Chapter One and other elementary and secondary education act programs have had little impact on the educational progress of the five million children served, despite expenditure of tens of billions of dollars over the years." That sentence could just as easily be applied to the entire Department of Education.

18

Money Alone is Not the Answer

But it's not just federal money that has been ineffectual. The U.S. as a whole, including states and localities, spends some $275 billion a year on public education. *Time* magazine reports, "The U.S. spends a greater percentage of its gross national product on education (7.5 percent) than any other country except Israel, and yet is outperformed in math and science by more than ten nations, including Hungary, Taiwan, and the former Soviet Union."[8] The ten states in the nation that rank highest in education performance, oddly enough, do not rank at the top in per-pupil expenditures. Money doesn't matter per se, because the very fact it is being spent does not mean it is helping kids. Less than half of federal education dollars go to pay for classroom instruction. Instead, the funds get eaten up by bureaucracies. Some estimate that 48.5 percent of the Chapter One money received by Washington, D.C., schools is spent on administration, including a "summer institute" for Board of Education members in the Solomon Islands and a variety of other dubious activities that do little to help students.

Strong Families, Strong Schools

Education depends on many other, more important things, especially involved, responsive, and loving parents. A study just released by the Department of Education called "Strong Families, Strong Schools," confirms the common-sense belief that parental involvement in education brings higher student performance. There is no substitute for parents. They are the ones most concerned about their children's education and who have the most

19

reliable sense of what will serve them best. According to a report by the National Education Commission on Time and Learning, U.S. students spend just 41 percent of their school day on math, geography, science, and other traditional academic courses. In contrast, students in countries such as Japan are spending at least twice as much time on these essentials.

Parents also know the importance of moral values. Rather than handing out condoms and promoting homosexuality, providing psychological counseling without parental consent, and pushing the skewed values of Outcome Based Education, schools should be reinforcing the values taught in homes, churches, and synagogues.

Education has traditionally been a local affair for other reasons. A parent can easily go to a meeting of the local school board or even run for a seat. Making it to the next meeting of the National Education Standards and Improvement Council is a dicier matter. A parent can walk into the office of his or her child's principal with relative ease. Finding the bureaucrat who administers federal regulations that determine what the school teaches is a nearly impossible task, and surely a futile one in any case. The further decisions are removed from local communities, the less influence community members will have on their communities. Locally based schools empower parents; federally influenced ones disenfranchise them. According to a *Wall Street Journal*/NBC News poll in December 1994, 72 percent of respondents said states should be given more responsiblity over education, while only 22 percent wanted more control for the federal government.

A first step in that process would be to abolish the Department of Education, the nexus for interest groups and bureaucrats. A whole range of spending programs could be cut out entirely, such as some of those included in *ESEA:* Arts in Education, the Eisenhower Professional Development Program, Women's Educational Equity Fund for Improvement of Education, and Eisenhower Professional Development Federal Activities. Programs such as student loans and antidiscrimination enforcement could be preserved and moved to other departments. The biggest spending programs, such as elementary and secondary education programs, could be converted into block grants and sent straight back to the states and localites.

Goals 2000, meanwhile, should simply be repealed. The savings from scrapping the department could be handed directly back to families in tax cuts or go to deficit reduction. With these changes, our schools would no longer be entrusted to distant government officials, but to people we know can make the grade: localities and, more importantly, American families.

3

Promoting School Choice

Enactment of legislation that will enhance parents' choice of schools for their children.

AMERICA'S PUBLIC SCHOOL SYSTEM once epitomized what was right about America. It was the showcase for our commitment to democracy. It was an engine fueling our economic growth. And it promised to provide a unified and thriving nation built by future generations who had shared the common experience of quality learning. Parents saw their children off to school confident that they were on their way to a better life.

Today, however, millions believe this vision of America has failed. Proficiency in even the most basic learning skills has declined alarmingly, threatening the nation's competitiveness and eroding our children's prospects for a prosperous future. Every year, students graduate even though they cannot read, write, or hope to meet future challenges. Hundreds of thousands drop out of school, leaving behind classmates who face terrifying violence and widespread apathy where once there was order and achievement. And despite record levels of public school spending, differences in the schools of the rich and poor remain vast.

Seeking Alternatives to Public Schools

Confronted by declining student performance, dangerous classrooms, and deteriorating school facilities, more and more parents are seeking an alternative. Those who can afford to do so have either moved to districts with better schools or placed their children in private and parochial institutions. But the majority of Americans remain trapped in a monopolistic system of mediocrity. Unable to afford private tuition or the housing costs of more affluent communities, most Americans have no choice but to send their children to schools selected not by them but by the education establishment. These schools, assured of both funding and immunity from market pressures, continue to operate in a manner that seems designed to satisfy education bureaucrats at the expense of student achievement.

And there is one more source of despair—the dire warnings of the federal government's 1983 report, *A Nation At Risk*, which have been almost completely ignored. In that landmark study, the National Commission on Excellence in Education made a startling statement:

> If an unfriendly foreign power had attempted to impose on America the mediocre educational performance that exists today, we might well have viewed it as an act of war. As it stands, we have allowed this to happen to ourselves. . . . We have, in effect, been committing an act of unthinking unilateral disarmament.[1]

Even worse, the school system described by the commission in 1983 was actually *better* than the one in operation today—despite the expenditure of $2 *trillion* on education spending in the intervening years.

Not surprisingly, the nation's public school system has received considerable scrutiny in the past few decades. But little in the way of substantive reform has been achieved. It seems that test scores cannot plummet enough to compel the education establishment to take the action that parents everywhere know is absolutely necessary.

Fueling the Education Revolution

In fact, the one factor that is most closely associated with America's education crisis—the bloated and unresponsive nature of the education bureaucracy—has become even more entrenched over time. The public school system is far more centralized today than at any time in the nation's history. After World War II, school funding and control moved from communities to regional school districts and from there to state agencies. Since then, the number of non-faculty staff members—people who do not teach our children—has swelled to unprecedented levels.[2] What have all these people been doing? It's hard to say, since at the same time the education bureaucracy was ballooning in size, student enrollment actually decreased.[3]

Given the state of public education in America today, it is easy to see why frustration has been replaced by fury in the minds of millions of parents. And why the call for educational *revolution* has been gaining strength.

School choice initiatives are sweeping the nation. Sixty-two percent of Americans favor choice among public schools, and 50 percent favor vouchers.[4] School choice legislation was either introduced or pending in thirty-four states in 1993.[5] These initiatives take a number of forms, including voucher programs, tax credits, and charter schools.

This is a nation fired by the spirit of competition. That the public education system has sacrificed student performance for the sake of centralized control contradicts our heritage. It stands to reason that excellence in education will only be achieved when schools are freed from their bureaucratic constraints to compete for students on the basis of quality instruction. That is the guiding principle of school choice.

Offering Students a Choice

School choice is a simple concept that offers extraordinary benefits. In essence, choice gives parents an equal opportunity to secure a quality education for their children. No longer would mobility and well-funded public schools be a luxury enjoyed only by the wealthy. In a typical choice system, students would receive scholarships or vouchers that they could use to enroll at the public or private school of their choice.

As a result, parents would be empowered to again play a central role in one of the most important phases of their children's lives. Because it gives families the freedom to choose where their children will attend school, choice restores to parents the vital role that school bureaucrats have assumed in recent decades.

Since families would decide where they wanted to direct their children's education dollars, choice creates a compelling incentive for all schools, public and private, to become fully responsive to the desires of students and their parents. Families unhappy with the school in which they are currently enrolled would be free to transfer to one that better meets their needs, thus making all schools more accountable for the education, safety, and achievement of their students.

Would school choice be as effective as promised? Perhaps the best answer can be found simply by taking a look at our system of colleges and universities. Because they depend on student enrollment for financial survival, they have developed high-quality academic programs and rewarding social environments in order to attract students. Competition has made them all better. And since recipients of government loans and grants can attend any college they wish—public, private, or religious—an extensive form of school choice already exists. The result is a higher education system widely hailed as the best in the world.

By contrast, America's public primary and secondary schools win few such accolades. No matter how poorly public schools perform, low-income parents and students are locked in. The lesson is clear. In order for America's children to enjoy the same quality instruction provided to their college-bound elders, public schools must compete for students on the basis of performance.

Competition Improves Education

Today, public schools labor under the crushing weight of excessive bureaucratic control. School choice removes this obstacle to education excellence simply by making use of the free market. In a competitive system of education, control is decentralized to the lowest possible level because the effort to attract students becomes the responsibility of individual schools. As is the case in the private sector, successful schools would likely do without bureaucrats altogether rather than permit the growth of a cumbersome and costly bureaucracy. Instead, they would form teams of parents, teachers, and principals to create the best learning environment possible.

In essence, choice frees schools from the bureaucracy that so often chokes innovation with a micromanaged maze of rules and regulations. It gives teachers and principals the freedom to do what they do best—teach. And it gives parents a central role in the operation of their school and the education of their children.

In fact, the key to school choice is the role that it permits families to play as education consumers. Empowered to spend their education dollars at the school of their choice, students and parents would quickly shun schools that are academically inferior, personally unresponsive, and operationally deficient. Instead, they would choose schools that are more rewarding, welcoming, and dedicated to student education.

One of the most important ways in which choice would improve the quality of our schools is by improving the quality of school personnel. Too often today, success in the teaching profession has little relation to actual competence as a teacher. A teacher's salary, benefits, and job security are largely dependent upon seniority, not ability. Under a competitive system of school choice, this would soon change. In order for schools to attract students, they would have to improve the quality of their instruction. As a result, they would have a strong incentive to hire and promote teachers solely on the basis of merit. Rather than allow teachers and administrators to advance despite their school's poor performance, choice would reward innovative and competent professionals while replacing their underperforming colleagues. And where bureaucratic costs currently squeeze teacher compensation, choice would place quality teachers and their salaries where they belong: at the top of the education pyramid.[6]

Offering Curricula Choices

Another important benefit of school choice would be its impact on school curricula. Today, public schools tend to offer a limited range of courses that does not give students the room to grow as individuals. Worse still, a number of schools have adopted politically correct curricula that do not correspond to either the academic needs or the personal values of students and their parents. Under choice, schools would specialize in order to attract students. By complementing traditional instruction with new programs designed to meet the broad range of student interests, schools would focus upon the subject areas desired by their students. Examples of specialized school curricula could include computer science, the performing arts, advanced languages, and even business management. In effect, choice would convert virtually all public schools into successful charter schools—alternative schools chartered and funded by states to meet the needs of a diverse student population.

In this way, choice would ensure the satisfaction of personal preferences. All across America, debates continue to rage over issues that concern the education of our children. Ranging from school prayer and sex education to dress codes and cultural emphasis, these issues often create great turmoil in families and schools alike. So long as the public school system remains monopolistic in nature, these debates will not be resolved to the satisfaction of all concerned. As a result, the current system's adoption of a single rigid approach to education frustrates and drives a significant number of students into private schools. By adopting a more decentralized and responsive approach to education, however, choice would permit families with differing personal preferences to enroll in public and private schools that reflect their interests. As a result of its embrace of diversity, choice would convert today's source of conflict into the basis for a broad range of school specialization.

Ensuring Equity for Disadvantaged Students

It is as a result of this flexibility that choice would also ensure greater educational equity for the millions of American students who are poor, of a racial or ethnic minority, or have special needs. School choice promotes equity by giving all such students the same mobility as their wealthier classmates. Today, many poor and middle class families not only live in districts with low per-pupil funding and particularly bad schools, they are also often unable to move to better districts or afford private or parochial education. For example, unlike the Clintons (who send their daughter, Chelsea, to a prestigious private school), most families living in Washington, D.C., cannot afford to escape the low performance and high crime of neighborhood public schools. This is particularly true of those District residents who, like the Clintons, live in public housing. As a result, the current system actively discriminates against low-income families.[7]

School choice would also deal a death blow to inequities related to race. Current public school policy dictates that students attend the school in the closest geographic vicinity to their home. Since a number of American communities remain somewhat segregated, area public schools tend to be similarly polarized. School choice breaks the link between residential patterns and school enrollment, however, thereby promising greater integration. In a system of choice, students would enroll in schools chosen not on the basis of their street address but on the basis of quality. Because the desire to get a good education is shared by all Americans, classrooms would be populated by students sharing only the desire to attend the school in which they enrolled. As Professor Ben Chavis, an American Indian teaching at San Francisco State University, describes it, "choice empowers and empowerment eliminates discrimination."[8]

Finally, students with special needs would also enjoy greater freedom. Education policy experts and the press have long documented the difficulty that public schools have in meeting the needs of learning disabled students. At present, the education of challenged children is hampered by the inability of public schools to give them the special attention they need. Likewise, gifted students are often bored by the standardized level of instruction provided in public schools. Like their learning disabled classmates, gifted students need specially tailored instruction. Under school choice, families with learning disabled and gifted children would be free to enroll them in schools that specialize in programs that meet their special needs.[9]

Freedom from Violence

A glance at daily newspapers, however, tells us that freedom is not just an issue of equity. For too many of our children today, the freedom they most desire is freedom from in-school violence. The tragedy of school-based crime is not just that it takes place. The real tragedy is that those who suffer its effects are actually victimized twice: once by the students whose violent acts threaten the safety and learning ability of our children, and then by the public school system that has done too little to crack down on school-based crime. The victims of such crime are in the one place where their families assume they will be safe. The epidemic of school violence, however, has made many public schools places where safety and nurturing are but fond memories. Even worse, the school system that has failed to eradicate crime also prevents all but wealthy students from moving to safer schools.

Here, too, school choice would likely have a significant impact. By empowering families to select the school they consider best, choice would permit students to leave schools in which crime is a major problem. As a result, schools that have yet to muster the determination necessary to control student violence would have a compelling reason to do so. Better still, the schools to which students would transfer—be they public or private, new or old—would be far less likely to experience criminal activity. In a system of choice, students would be attending the schools they want to attend. And student satisfaction and fulfillment is perhaps the most effective weapon against school-based crime.

Increasing Parental Involvement

Of all the arguments supporting school choice, however, perhaps the most compelling is that it will increase the level of parental involvement in the education of their children. Today, parental involvement in public schools is the exception rather than the rule. The current public school system, from local school boards to state departments of education, tends to be alarmingly unresponsive to the opinions and objectives of parents. As a result, the role of the parent has been reduced to an all-time low. As the nation's governors observed in a 1986 report of the National Governors Association,

> [T]oo often, parents of students in the public school system recognize that they have no choice, and they reason that they have no responsibility. They assume that a societal institution called public school in their neighborhood has a monopoly on the education of their children. Our model of compulsory, packaged education, as it now exists, is an enemy of parental involvement and responsibility simply because it allows no choice.[10]

One certain effect of school choice is that parents would again have a real stake in the schools their children attend. Granted the right to choose the best school for their children, parents would be able to assert a stronger role in the schools they select. It is a fundamental element of human nature that people care more about the events in which they are personally involved. Since school choice relies upon the direct participation of families, all of the schools in which students would enroll would enjoy the level of parental involvement and enthusiasm enjoyed almost solely by private schools today.

The ability of choice to increase parental involvement is evident in the few districts where choice has been permitted. In fact, in these cities, choice energized far more parental interest and involvement than had been anticipated. For example, when a small-scale privately funded voucher program was established in Indianapolis, organizers hoped that one hundred or two hundred families would apply. Instead, more than six hundred applications were received just in the first three days of the program's operation. Milwaukee's school choice program became so popular that inner city parents formed a waiting list and even filed a lawsuit to expand the program. And in the New York City borough of East Harlem, a choice program that is now in its third decade has made parents so integral to school operations that they help design curriculum, rate teachers, and administer the schools. Clearly, when parents have been presented with the opportunity to become involved in the education of their children, they have responded enthusiastically.

The experience of school choice initiatives, unfortunately, suggests that enthusiasm may not be enough. Recognizing that the nation's public school system will not be fundamentally improved until its bureaucratic system of centralized control is dismantled, the education labor unions continue to fight school choice vigorously. As a result, the challenge facing concerned families nationwide is to fight for incremental change as the first step down the road to real reform.

Enacting School Choice Legislation

Two bills currently before the 104th Congress offer what may be the most promising opportunity for reform yet to face the nation. These measures—H.R. 1640, sponsored by Reps. Frank Riggs (R-Calif.) and Dave Weldon (R-Fla.), and S. 618, sponsored by Senators Dan Coats (R-Ind.) and Joseph Lieberman (D-Conn.)—would establish demonstration projects in up to twenty low-income communities. Under these plans, families whose children are eligible for the federal school lunch program would receive vouchers with which to send their children to the public, private, or parochial school of their choice.

These bills have the potential to initiate a nationwide school choice movement. Because one of the provisions calls for a complete evaluation of the results of the demonstration projects, this legislation could help defeat any remaining opposition to choice. Indeed, should this limited foray into enhanced parental involvement prove effective, there will no longer remain any substantive reason for blocking school choice from families all across the nation.

It is for this reason that the enactment of legislation enhancing parental choice of their children's schools is one of the ten provisions of the *Contract for the American Family*. Christian Coalition strongly supports the swift passage of school choice legislation such as H.R. 1640 and S. 618 during the 104th Congress. Only by adopting such common-sense reform efforts as H.R. 1640 and S. 618 can we energize the strong grass-roots support that is needed to make better schools and brighter futures a reality for all of our children.

4

Protecting Parental Rights

Enactment of a Parental Rights Act *and defeat of the* UN Convention on the Rights of the Child.

ALTHOUGH PARENTAL RIGHTS and family freedoms are firmly established as fundamental and beyond the reach of any court, lower courts and agencies have not prevented wholesale invasions of homes and families. Parental rights are under attack, and families across the nation are being harmed by a legal system that refuses to protect their fundamental rights.

A number of important issues face parents and their ability to raise their children free from governmental interference. One is found in the *Parental Rights Act of 1995* and the other is found in the *UN Convention on the Rights of the Child*.

Lower Courts Limiting Parents' Rights

The *Parental Rights Act of 1995* (PRA) reaffirms the rights of parents to direct the upbringing of their children. While most parents assume this right is protected, some lower courts and government bureaucrats have acted to limit this basic freedom. Senator Chuck Grassley (R-Iowa) stepped into the battle to protect the family from unwarranted intrusions by the government, and with assistance from the Home School Legal Defense Association, is preparing legislation that will protect parental rights. Congressmen Steve Largent (R-Okla.) and Mike Parker (D-Miss.) have joined Senator Grassley to champion this legislative initiative for the American family.

While the Constitution does not explicitly address the parent-child relationship, the Supreme Court clearly regards the right of parents to direct the upbringing of their children as a fundamental right under the Fourteenth Amendment to the United States Constitution. Fundamental rights, such as freedom of speech and religion, have always received the highest legal protection.

Two cases in the 1920s affirmed the court's high regard for the integrity of the parent-child relationship. In *Meyer v. Nebraska*,[1] a Nebraska teacher was convicted under a state law for teaching German to a ten-year-old child. The court held that his right to teach and the right of the parents to hire him for that purpose were clearly within the liberty clause of the Fourteenth Amendment. The Court declared that the Fourteenth Amendment "[w]ithout doubt, . . . denotes not merely freedom from bodily restraint but also the right of the individual to . . . marry, establish a home and bring up children, to worship God according to the dictates of his own conscience. . . ."[2]

The second case of note is *Pierce v. Society of Sisters*.[3] In this case, Oregon passed a state law requiring that all children, ages eight to sixteen years, be educated in public schools, which effectively outlawed private and religious education for children. The court declared that "[in] this day and under our civilization, the child of man is his parent's child and not the State's. . . . It is not seriously debatable that the parental right to guide one's child intellectually and religiously is a most substantial part of the liberty and freedom of the parent."[4] The court went on to hold that parents are chiefly responsible for the education and upbringing of their children.

While the Supreme Court's intent to protect parental rights is unquestionable, lower courts have not always followed this high standard to protect the parent-child relationship. The recent lower court assault on the rights of parents to direct their children's education, medical decisions, and discipline is unprecedented. Imagine yourself in the following real-life, documented situations.

Courts Reject Parents' Right to Know

In the first case, a group of parents in Chelmsford, Massachusetts, sued when their children were required to sit through a ninety-minute AIDS awareness presentation by "Hot, Sexy, and Safer Productions, Inc." In this so-called "group sexual experience" students were told to play explicit sex games with condoms.[5] When the students' parents challenged the propriety of the school's actions, the court held that the parents, who were never told about the presentation, did not have a right to know and consent to this sexually explicit program before their children were required to attend.

In the second case, the Ohio Supreme Court took children out of the custody of a "fit and good mother with normal, delightful children" solely because she had chosen to conduct a legal home school program.[6] While Mrs.

Gardini was approved by the state in her application to home school her children, a court-appointed psychologist testified that the effects of homeschooling upon the children caused losses in "socialization" and "normalization" development.[7] The court decided it was in the best interests of the children to remove custody from the homeschooling mother.

Who Sets the Rules at Home?

Imagine losing custody of your child because your idea of discipline is different than a state social worker. The Washington State Supreme Court ruled that it was not a violation of parents' rights to remove an eighth-grade child from her family because she objected to the ground rules established in the home. The parents in this case grounded their daughter because she wanted to smoke marijuana and sleep with her boyfriend. She objected, and the courts removed her from the home.[8] While most parents would consider these rules imminently reasonable, the court held that although the family structure is a fundamental institution of our society, and parental perogatives are entitled to considerable legal deference, they are not absolute and must yield to fundamental rights of the child or important interests of the state.[9]

Recent news accounts reported the case of a father who was accused of child abuse because he publicly spanked his four-year-old daughter. When she deliberately slammed the car door on her brother's hand, her father acted promptly to discipline her by a reasonably administered spanking. A passer-by called the police and the father had to defend against the charge of child abuse. While the father won his case, it is amazing to most parents that they could be dragged into court against their will to defend against such an outrageous charge of child abuse for disciplining their children for open rebellion.

Another outrageous example of the state meddling in the rightful decisions of a parent is Kevin, age fifteen, who had "elephant man disease," which caused a large fold of skin to grow over the right side of his face. Kevin's mother, a Jehovah's Witness, wanted to wait until Kevin turned twenty-one before permitting any cosmetic surgery. Doctors testified that the surgery was very risky and offered no cure, and that waiting would decrease the risk. The court, however, overruled the mother's objections, declaring Kevin a "neglected child," and ordered the operations.[10]

Unfortunately, these cases are only a few of the many examples of parents' rights being violated when trying to direct the training and nurturing of their children. If these were the only examples of the movement to violate parental rights, they would be bad enough. However, recent public debate has further fueled the need for clarifying language to protect parental rights.

A License for Parents?

In October 1994, Dr. Jack Westman of the University of the Wisconsin-Madison published a book entitled *Licensing Parents: Can We Prevent Child Abuse and Neglect?* Westman proposes that the state license parents as a means of conveying the seriousness of the parental responsibility. While there should be no question of the awesome responsibility to raise and nurture children, the idea of the state licensing potential parents for the right to have children raises many serious questions. Who will decide what will be the appropriate standards for parenthood? What values will drive these decisions? What if a potential parent does not qualify under the state licensing guidelines? What do we do when a woman becomes pregnant before she has been "licensed"? The very idea of licensing parents stretches the imagination of freedom-loving Americans.

Refuting Westman's concept of licensing parents, William Norman Grigg refers to the "[t]raditional American perspective on the family" rooted in the biblical principle of stewardship: Children belong to God, but they are the primary responsibility of parents.[11] This principle is one with which most parents agree. Unfortunately, it is clearly in question by many social scientists of our day.

A Question of Government Protection

Another phrase often heard in recent social debate is the old proverb that "it takes the whole village to raise a child." Former Surgeon General Jocelyn Elders and Attorney General of the United States Janet Reno have both quoted this proverb. While there is nothing innately wrong with the statement that a community should support the rearing of a child, it is critical that the parents be held chiefly responsible for decisions concerning children and the community play only a supportive role.

With recent lower court cases, the "parent licensing" movement, and the "village child rearing" debate as examples, it is easy to see the need for the *Parental Rights Act of 1995*.

The goal of the PRA is to reaffirm the parental right to direct the upbringing of children in four major areas: (1) directing or providing for the education of the child;

(2) making medical decisions for the child; (3) disciplining the child, including reasonable corporal discipline; and (4) directing or providing for the religious teaching of the child.

The *Parental Rights Act* would accomplish this goal by clarifying for lower courts and administrative tribunals that the proper standard to use in disputes between the government and parents is the highest legal standard available. This standard, known as "the compelling interest standard" means that before the government can interfere in the parent-child relationship, it must demonstrate that there is a "compelling" interest to protect and that the means the government is using to protect this interest is the "least restrictive" means available. Practically speaking, this means that the law in question is not so broad in application that it sweeps in more than is necessary to protect the interest in question.

An example will help to clarify this point. Television and newspaper accounts often detail instances of parents who have beaten their children or neglected their most basic needs for food and shelter. Clearly, protecting children from this kind of abuse or neglect would fit into a reasonable person's definition of a compelling interest of the state. One of the purposes of the *Parental Rights Act* would be to protect children from abuse and neglect as those terms have been traditionally defined and applied and to recognize that protecting children in these circumstances is an example of a compelling state interest. Abusing or neglecting a child has never been considered a protected parental right.

Using the "least restrictive" means available to protect children from abuse and neglect would mean that parents who meet these needs could not fall victim to the state law. The law would be written in such a way that it would cover parents who are abusing or neglecting their children but not cover parents who are not. If the law were written so poorly that even good, loving parents could be accused of child abuse, it would not pass the test of being the "least restrictive" means available and would have to be modified.

The *Parental Rights Act* reaffirms the Supreme Court perspective that parents have the right to direct the upbringing of their children. Further, it affirms that the proper legal standard for lower courts to use is the highest legal standard available for other fundamental rights like freedom of speech and freedom of religion.

The Parental Rights Act

Parents might ask, "How is the *Parental Rights Act* going to work?" It uses a process to evaluate fundamental rights which balances the interests of parents, children, and the government. First, parents are required to demonstrate that the actions being questioned are within their fundamental right to direct the upbringing of their children. Second, they must show that the government interfered with this right. If the parents are able to prove these two things, then the burden shifts to the government. The government must then show that the interference was essential to accomplish a compelling government interest and that the government's method of interfering was the least restrictive means to accomplish its goal.

In these cases, the court would balance the parents' right to make decisions on behalf of their children against the government's right to interfere in the family relationship and decide which was correct. While it would be better if lower courts and administrative agencies would use the appropriate legal standard outlined by the Supreme Court without congress having to clarify it, history shows this is not likely to occur.

Another of the grave threats to parents' rights in America comes from the *United Nations Convention on the Rights of the Child.*

A Serious Threat to Parental Rights

The *UN Convention on the Rights of the Child* was unanimously adopted by the General Assembly of the United Nations on November 20, 1989. The convention drafting process spanned ten years, during which the United States was an active participant. UNICEF targeted 1995 as the year for universal ratification. At this point, 176 nations, including the Vatican and virtually every major industrialized nation, are signatories to the convention. The United States is one of few nations that has not ratified the treaty.

President Clinton is being subjected to extraordinary international pressure from children's rights organizations. Over 150 groups have indicated their support for the *UN Convention on the Rights of the Child* and are urging him to send it to the Senate. These include the National Education Association, the National Council of Churches, the Children's Defense Fund, American Council for Social Services, the National Committee for the Rights of the Child, the National Council for Child's Rights, Planned Parenthood, International School of Psychology Association, the National School Board Association, the American

Bar Association, the International Council on Social Welfare, and more.

The path is set and the push has begun for the *UN Convention on the Rights of the Child* to be ratified by the U.S. Senate. When the President will send the treaty to the Senate is not known.

Were the treaty to be passed, it would pose a serious threat to parents' rights. In compliance with the treaty, the United States would be obligated to "ensure" various rights of children. Specifically, the U.S. would need to "ensure":

1. That every child shall be registered by the government immediately after birth (art. 7).
2. That every child shall receive the highest attainable level of health care services (art. 24).
3. That no child is subjected to corporal punishment. Article 28.2 states that all schools must be prohibited from using corporal punishment. In article 19.1, and in article 37 (a), it not only prohibits school authorities from administering corporal discipline, but it also applies it to "parents, legal guardians, or any other person who has care of the child."
4. Under the UN treaty, the United States will be required to ensure that children are vested with "freedom of expression." Section 1 states that a child has a right to "seek, receive and impart information of all kinds, regardless of frontiers, either orally in writing or in print, in the form of art, or through any other media of the child's choice." This essentially gives children the right to listen to rock music, watch tele-

vision, and possibly have access to pornography—no matter what their parents might say.

5. Furthermore, children are guaranteed the "freedom of thought, conscience, and religion." This could give children the right to object to their parents' religious training and participate in religious services of cults.

6. Under the treaty, the child would have the "right to freedom of association." Parents could be prevented from prohibiting their children from associating with certain other children or juvenile delinquents.

7. A child will be given a "right of privacy," which would open the door for children to get access to abortion over their parents' objection. This would virtually invalidate all parental notification laws concerning abortion, which have been passed in twenty-three states and enjoy support of 70 percent of the American people.

8. Howard Davidson, Director of the American Bar Association Center on Children and Law, and Cynthia Price Cohen, member of the Ad Hoc Non-Governmental Group on the Drafting of the Convention on the Rights of the Child, have written a treatise entitled, *Children's Rights in America:* UN Convention on the Rights of the Child *Compared with United States Law.*[12] In Article 29, the American Bar Association treatise by Cohen and Davidson indicates this article would force the public schools of America to adopt "federally prescribed curriculum content."[13] Furthermore, the curriculum would "prescribe certain values which the State Parties agree to transmit the children through education." Each child would be

required to be prepared to be a responsible citizen by having "the spirit of understanding, peace, toleration, equity of sexes, and friendship for all peoples, ethnic, national, and religious groups of indigenous origin" (art. 29).

Cohen and Davidson further comment, "It is conceivable that the court could someday move toward prescribing some values content in private school curriculum."[14] They assert that private schools "must conform to certain standards, specifically those enumerated in Article 29 and such minimum standards may be laid down by the state."[15] They specifically criticize curriculum used by Accelerated Christian Education (ACE) and the teaching in Bethany Baptist Academy in Illinois since their teachings of Christianity as the only true religion "flies in the face of Articles 29.1(b), (c), (d)."[16]

9. Under the treaty, governments must enforce the right of the child to "freely participate in cultural life and arts."[17]

It is clear from these few examples that this treaty would virtually undermine parents' rights as we know them in the United States. Parents no longer would have the basic right to control what their children watch on television, whom they associate with, and what church they attend.

The *UN Convention on the Rights of the Child* makes it clear that a new standard will prevail as to determining whether or not action taken for or against the child is proper. In article 3, section 1, the provision gives the state the power to make all decisions regarding the welfare of the child by divesting parents of their right to determine what is in the best interest of the child and transferring this right to government. The treaty states, "In all actions concerning children, whether undertaken by public or private social welfare institutions, courts of law, administrative authorities, or legislative bodies, the best interest of the child will be a primary consideration." The best interest of the child is a completely subjective standard which will be determined by social workers and not parents.

The treaty makes it clear that infringement on a child's rights could cause the parents to be prosecuted with the possibility of having the child removed from the home. This treaty, if it is ratified by the U.S. Senate and becomes the law of the land in the United States, will have to be balanced by the federal courts and will be used to empower children's rights advocates in our already uncontrollable welfare system. The rights which the treaty gives children are in direct opposition to those of those parents' rights and will cause untold litigation in our country.

The bottom line is that we do not need the *UN Convention on the Rights of the Child* in the United States. We already have a massive child welfare system in place throughout the country. The *UN Convention on the Rights of the Child* prohibits such things as slave labor of children. To be sure, this is of great significance in lesser developed nations, where the tragedy of child slave labor should be abolished, but in the United States it is not relevant. We do not need to sign this treaty to maintain our position as a world power, nor is our signing of this treaty necessary to influence other nations to clean up their human rights records for both adults and children. To sign the treaty for this purpose is completely illogical, especially when it poses such a terrible risk to the parental rights and free-doms of U.S. citizens.

Since the United States takes treaties seriously, we will have to implement these aspects of the treaty by the man-dates of our own Constitution under the Supremacy Clause. The treaty is better designed for nations such as China and Iraq. In fact, China willingly signed the treaty. However, it means nothing to China since China does not have any provisions in its constitution making treaties the supreme law of the land. It is purely cosmetic. Entering into a treaty of this type is virtually irrelevant for all those nations that most need to protect children to the degree we already do in the United States.

While discussions surrounding parental rights are some-times confusing, the simple truth is, they are vital. Whether it is through the defeat of the *UN Convention on the Rights of the Child* or through the enactment of the *Parental Rights Act,* Christian Coalition believes that con-cerned citizens should make known their support for the Parental Rights Act to their senators and congressmen. Without passage of the PRA, lower courts, government bureaucrats, and administrative tribunals will continue to interfere in the parent-child relationship when it is not necessary. This interference is a violation of the responsi-bility of stewardship for the child and of the basic right of the parent to direct the upbringing of the child.

5

Family-Friendly Tax Relief

Reduce the tax burden on the American family, eliminate the marriage penalty, and pass the Mother's and Homemaker's Rights Act *to remedy the unequal treatment that homemakers receive under the Internal Revenue Service Code with respect to saving for retirement.*

IT HAS BEEN SAID that the intact family is the most successful Department of Health, Education, and Welfare ever created. Of all society's institutions, none is as good as the family in meeting people's—wives', husbands', and children's—needs. Survey after survey and report after report come to the same conclusion: the family is the foundation of all human relationships and the foundation for every society.

Common sense would seem to dictate that government would do everything in its power to encourage both family formation and family stability. Or at the very least, that government would do everything it could to treat the family as fairly as every other societal institution. Unfortunately, that is not the case.

51

Unfair Taxes on the Family

Today, the American family is the most heavily taxed entity in the nation. Through its bewilderingly complex tax code that includes nearly five million words of regulations and explanations, the federal government has punished families that work, save, and stay together.

It is hard to overestimate our tax code's damage to American families. Many people look back to the 1950s and 1960s with nostalgia. At least with regard to the tax code, that nostalgia is understandable. Those were the days when one income was often all that was needed to support a family. Today, many families need two incomes just to pay taxes and meet basic needs. The postwar era marked the time when families were able to set aside money for their golden years. Today, the specter of unaffordable retirement faces millions of families who do not have the resources to spare for even minimal levels of saving. During the fifties and sixties, parents raised their children confident that they would be more prosperous than the generations that preceded them. Now post–Baby Boomers are beginning to believe that the American promise of prosperity has passed them by. Many will be unable to buy their first homes until later in life, and they will have much more difficulty putting their children through college than their parents did. Families find it harder and harder just to make ends meet.

Consider the following: In 1954, the average family of four paid just 2 percent of its adjusted gross income in federal income taxes. Today, that figure has soared to 25 percent.[1] When state and local taxes are added, the average family of four pays almost 40 percent of its entire

52

income in taxes. That unbelievable amount is more than families spend on such essentials as housing, clothing, and food—combined.[2]

Busy Parents, Lonely Children

Clearly, the American family needs relief, and it needs it now. To a very large extent, the economic and personal challenges facing families today are rooted in the consequences of America's system of taxation. The strain of meeting America's crushing tax burden has forced many homemakers into the work force, reducing the amount of time that parents spend with their children by approximately one-half. Parents spend about 40 percent fewer hours with their children than parents did just a generation ago. And almost 20 percent of teenagers have not had a high-quality conversation of more than ten minutes with either one of their parents in at least a month.

The net effect of this? Perhaps the preeminent Harvard psychiatrist Robert Coles put it best: "Parents are too busy spending their most precious capital—their time and their energy—struggling to keep up with MasterCard payments. . . . They work long hours to barely keep up, and when they get home at the end of the day they're tired. And their kids are left with a Nintendo or a pair of Nikes. . . . Big deal." What has caused this situation? An overbearing tax system.

This is not how parents want to live and not how parents want to raise their children. A 1989 *New York Times* survey reported that 83 percent of working mothers felt torn between the financial need to work and their personal desire to spend more time with their families.[3] A 1990 *Los Angeles Times* poll found that 57 percent of all fathers and

55 percent of all mothers feel guilty about not spending enough time with their kids. A 1988 *USA Today* survey found that 73 percent of two-income families would prefer that one parent remain at home to care for their children if money were not a factor.[4]

Perhaps the most disturbing thing about this dramatic loss of family time is the fact that the second income does little to improve family financial well-being. In fact, approximately two-thirds of a working mother's income is consumed solely by the family's federal tax liability.[5] Unless the tax burden on families is reduced, working-parent families will continue to see one of their two incomes supporting government, not the family.

Taxes that Penalize Families

The rise in the family tax burden is due to a number of factors. One is the remarkable increase in the size and scope of government. In just the past few decades government has grown from spending about $400 per capita to well over $11,000 per capita in constant dollars. It has grown from about six million employees to nearly nineteen million. And it has increased its debt by more than $3 trillion dollars.

In its unprecedented growth, government has had to find revenue somewhere. That somewhere has been in the family. The federal tax structure utilizes two schedules, one for single individuals and another for married couples. The net effect of the differing tax treatment is substantial, with married couples bearing a greater tax burden that do their unmarried counterparts. For example, a two-parent family in which both parents work and earn a total of $30,000 annually will pay more than $1,600 in federal taxes. By contrast, an unmarried couple with children and the same income would actually receive a tax refund of almost $600. Worse still, if only one member of the married couple is working, the federal tax liability almost doubles.

Another important factor in the crushing family tax burden is the eroded value of the personal and dependent tax exemptions. Intended to offset part of the annual cost of raising a child, the dependent exemption has not kept pace with inflation. Like the personal exemption, the dependent tax exemption has a much smaller value today relative to total income than it did in past decades. In 1948, the tax exemption for a child was $600 and offset more than 42 percent of per capita income. If the exemption had retained its value, it would now equal approximately $9,200. Instead, it is worth only $2,500 and offsets less than 12 percent of today's average per capita income.[6]

Related to the change in tax exemptions, of course, is the rise in individual income tax rates and the increased Social Security and Medicare payroll tax burden. These "payroll taxes" have skyrocketed. In 1948, all workers paid about two percent of annual wages up to $3,000 on Social Security tax; 1 percent was paid directly by the employee and 1 percent indirectly by the employer through the so-called employer share. But that has changed. In 1992, the combined Social Security taxes ate up more than 15 percent on wages up to $55,500.

While the increases in these taxes have certainly affected all workers, they have had a far more profound effect on working families with children. The reason for this is that Social Security taxes, unlike standard income taxes, are not adjusted for the number of dependents in the family. The net effect of this is that a working parent trying to support a family of four feels the sting of this tax far more sharply than a single person at the same wage level. This is particularly true of lower income parents. A family with an income of $25,000 per year, for instance, pays $3,750 in payroll taxes.

To put all of this in some additional perspective, total pretax income for the median family of four in 1992 was $47,787. As Scott Hodge of The Heritage Foundation points out, after taxes are taken out, that family's income fell to $36,915. If federal taxes as a percentage of family income were restored to 1948 levels, the family's post-tax income would have been $10,060 higher, or $46,975. In other words, the loss of income in 1992 because of the increase in federal taxes as a share of family income, due to the falling value of the personal exemption and the rise in Social Security taxes since the late 1940s, was $10,060.

This income loss severely affects the ability of families to support themselves. The median price of a single-family home purchased in 1992, for instance, was $103,700. The average annual mortgage payment on such a home (including principal and interest) was $7,380. Thus, the annual family income loss due to increased federal tax rates for the average family in the last four decades actually exceeds the annual cost of an average home mortgage by 36 percent.

Where once these taxes consumed a small percentage of a limited share of income, today the tax rates and the level of income subject to taxation have both increased. In fact, this year Tax Freedom Day—the day when the average American's income is no longer completely consumed by federal, state, and local taxes—did not arrive until May 6.[7]

Discouraging Saving and Investing

It gets worse. Just as tax rates and exemptions have had a serious impact on the American family, the tax code also poses a grave threat to the economy as a whole. For example, the current tax code discourages savings and investment—the two ingredients necessary for thriving economic growth. Individuals who wish to save for future needs are taxed twice, once when they earn the income they plan to save and again when those savings reap interest. Likewise, investment income is taxed two times. Corporations pay an income tax on earnings realized from investment, as do individual investors when they receive the increased dividends that successful investments typically produce. It is little wonder then that America's savings and investment rates are far lower than is needed to preserve the economic vitality that helped build this nation.

Nor is it at all surprising that many companies cite the federal tax code as a primary reason for moving their factories overseas. After all, the companies that remain in America not only have to face the direct costs of tax liability, they also have to shoulder the expense of complying with the unbelievably complex tax code. When the University of Michigan surveyed 1,300 large companies in 1993, it found that each company spent an average of $1.6 million to comply with the tax code. In other words, nearly $2.1 billion dollars that could have been used by those companies to hire more workers, increase wages, or invest in future productivity were wasted. All told, it is estimated that as much as a half-trillion dollars may be lost annually to compliance costs and other productivity disincentives.[8]

All this means a tighter job market offering lower wages. When the impact of payroll taxes, disincentives for savings and investment, and the cost of complying with the tax code is considered, it is not hard to see why many families feel financially pressed. Whatever the intentions behind the unprecedented rise in our income and payroll taxes, the outcome has been nothing short of disastrous. The lesson is clear: When taxes rise, families lose.

A glance at the history of income taxation in America bears this out. For more than thirty-five years, federal income tax revenues have rarely risen above or dropped below 20 percent of America's Gross Domestic Product (GDP). This may not seem important, but it should be recalled that since 1960, the top tax rate has been as high as 91 percent and as low as 28 percent. No matter where income tax rates have been set, total revenues have barely budged.[9]

The "secret" behind the income tax is that people do not like paying it. This may seem completely obvious, but the Republican-led 104th Congress may be the first one to realize it. When taxes go up, taxpayers with the sophistication and resources to avoid paying taxes do so.[10] With the help of attorneys and accountants, they figure out a way to reduce their tax liability.

Since taxes have gone up far more often than they have dropped, however, tax avoidance has remained a profitable business. It is, unfortunately, an activity in which the average American family does not engage. Unable to afford the high-priced help needed to master the tax code, families with moderate incomes cannot avoid a significant tax increase. Advocates of tax increases have it all wrong: whenever a politician talks about soaking the rich, it is the average American family that drowns in red ink.

Tax Relief for Families

As dire as the situation may appear, the risk of financial immersion that has long threatened millions of families finally appears to be ebbing. As part of its Contract with America, the Republican-led House of Representatives passed the *American Dream Restoration Act.* Among its provisions is the *Tax Fairness and Deficit Reduction Act,* a collection of measures intended to permit Americans of all ages to keep more of their own income.

This tax relief bill, which is responsive to the needs of hard-pressed families, includes many of the provisions of the *Contract with the American Family.* If passed by the Senate and signed into law by President Clinton, it will grant families with incomes below $200,000 an annual child tax credit of $500 per child. In addition, it will protect eligible married couples from the impact of the tax code's marriage penalty by rebating up to $145 of their tax liability to them. The bill also encourages adoptions and parental care by giving adoptive parents a $5,000 tax credit and families that care for elderly parents a $500 credit.

Also central to the *Contract with the American Family* is the tax relief bill's inclusion of the *Mother's and Homemaker's Rights Act.* Like S. 287, a bill sponsored by Senators Kay Bailey Hutchison (R-Tex.) and Barbara Mikulski (D-Md.), the House of Representatives' tax relief bill reverses an important inequity of current Individual Retirement Account policy. The tax code has long permitted working individuals to make tax-deductible contributions to their IRAs. However, married couples were treated differently depending upon their employment status. Although two-income families were permitted to contribute up to $4,000 per year toward retirement, families in which one spouse worked as a homemaker were restricted to a total tax-deductible contribution of $2,250.

This inequity in the tax code reflects a disrespect for the valued role of homemakers. In response, both the tax relief bill and its Senate counterpart permit homemakers to receive tax-preferred treatment for IRA contributions of up to $2,000. This important reform should be complemented by indexing tax-deductible IRA contributions to inflation so that the value of families' joint retirement funds will not be eroded.

As promising as these measures are, they are only a beginning. The *American Dream Restoration Act* has been approved by the House of Representatives and awaits passage in the Senate. Meanwhile, the *Mother's and Homemaker's Rights Act* must be passed by both the House and the Senate. And, of course, both measures require the signature of President Clinton in order to take effect.

It is essential to the strengthening of American families that these bills be passed and signed into law. Just as important, success for these measures will turn the nation's attention to the critical task of fundamentally revising the Internal Revenue Code. It is for that reason that Christian Coalition supports the concept of a flatter tax structure with a generous exemption for children. Such a tax would achieve the ultimate goal of pro-family tax reform: a tax code that rewards work, savings, and investment while reducing the tax liability that has long burdened the American family. Only with such reform can we hope to remove the final financial obstacles to strong families and a prosperous future.

6

Restoring Respect for Human Life

Protecting the rights of states that do not fund abortion, protecting innocent human life by placing real limits on late-term abortions, and ending funds to organizations that promote and perform abortions.

THE FOUNDERS OF OUR NATION began by proclaiming, near the start of the Declaration of Independence, that they considered certain truths to be self-evident: "that all men are created equal, that they are endowed by their Creator with certain inalienable rights, that among these are Life, Liberty, and the pursuit of Happiness."

The right to life is, indeed, the bedrock on which all other rights rest. The framers of our Constitution explicitly protected a panoply of important personal and political liberties, including the right to speak freely, to express our religious faith, and to due process of law. But the one-and-a-half million unborn children who annually have their lives ended by legalized abortion will never enjoy these blessings of liberty, nor the pursuit of happiness.

As Mother Teresa said to those assembled for the National Prayer Breakfast in February 1994—President Clinton among them—"The greatest destroyer of peace today is abortion. It is a war against the child, a direct killing of the innocent child."[1] For Mother Teresa, as for all of those who recognize as undeniable the humanity of unborn children, abortion can never be regarded as merely a private matter.

Recognition of the sanctity of human life within the womb is a fundamental component of the Judeo-Christian ethic. Indeed, sanctions against abortion have been part of most human societies for thousands of years. An eminent historian of law and ethics, John T. Noonan, Jr., wrote that abhorrence for abortion is "an almost absolute value in human history."[2]

Abortions Are Increasing

Only in recent times have there been systematic attempts to legitimize abortion within Western systems of laws and medical ethics. The result has been an enormous increase in the total number of abortions performed. We have also seen the rapid development of grisly new methodologies and instruments that have made abortion technically feasible—and practiced—later and later into pregnancy.

Until 1967, the laws in all fifty states allowed for abortion only in those rare cases in which the mother's life was in danger. According to careful extrapolations, there were less than 200,000 abortions a year in the U.S. during this period (less than 10,000 of these being performed legally).[3]

By 1972, however, New York, California, and several other states had adopted laws allowing abortion on demand, and the number of *legal* reported abortions had already increased to 586,760.[4]

In January 1973, the U.S. Supreme Court handed down its *Roe v. Wade* ruling, which declared abortion to be a "fundamental right" under the Constitution. Within a few years, the overall abortion rate began to rise dramatically.

The first year after *Roe*, the number of reported abortions was 744,600. By 1975, it was more than one million. The number continued to climb sharply until the mid-1980s, when it reached 1.6 million.[5] The number is now about 1.5 million.

This enormously increased loss of human life to abortion would not have occurred without the Supreme Court's disastrous exercise in social engineering by judicial fiat. The law is an important teacher, and for a generation now, our law has taught that unborn human beings are disposable.

As a result, abortion is increasingly employed as a primary method of birth control. Half of the women seeking abortions each year now acknowledge at least one previous abortion, and this "repeater" rate is growing annually. One major study found that half of the women seeking abortions acknowledged that neither she nor her partner was using any conception-prevention method in the *month* during which the conception occurred. At a 1993 professional workshop, one abortion clinic worker described a client who had procured fourteen abortions, while another told of a woman who had received three second-trimester abortions in less than eighteen months.[6]

The human mind cannot grasp the reality of one-and-one-half million abortions. We must remind ourselves often that the statistic is made up of *individual* human beings whose lifespans are deliberately cut short. Each of us recognizes our own uniqueness, our own individuality, our own "personhood." Each of us also recognizes that our existence, as individuals, began not at birth, but at the time of our individual conceptions.

And surely, each one of us can say, "If my individual life had been cut off before birth, no other human being—even another child born later to the same parents—could possibly ever have been the unique individual who is *me*."

We should extend this same recognition to each and every unborn child. It is not the exact stage of development that matters, but the human individuality. Not one of these unborn individuals is repeatable. Not one is interchangeable with anyone else who came before or who will come after. None of them is expendable. They are our brothers and sisters in the human family—and we each were once, as they are now.

Respect for the right to life of each innocent individual human being is at the core of the Judeo-Christian ethic and of our political system as well. Therefore, Christian Coalition seeks by all lawful and nonviolent means to protect that right to life. We look forward to the day when the humanity and right to life of the unborn child is recognized by all people of good will, and is once again reflected in our laws and social norms.

A Separate Class of Human Beings

Our Constitution already guarantees the right to life. But at the moment, a majority of the members of the U.S. Supreme Court have cast unborn children beyond the reach of that protection. In *Roe v. Wade*, the Supreme Court has in effect amended the Constitution by judicial

66

decree, leaving a class of human beings open to violent assault.

In the 1992 *Planned Parenthood v. Casey* case, the Supreme Court reviewed its 1973 *Roe v. Wade* ruling—and reaffirmed it. The majority of justices did not examine and rebut the evidence of the humanity of unborn children, nor did they focus on the violence to human individuals that abortion is. Instead, they said that *Roe* must be reaffirmed, because "a decision to overrule *Roe*'s essential holding under the existing circumstances would address error, if error there was, at the cost of both profound and unnecessary damage to the Court's legitimacy."

In addition, the justices wrote,

> for two decades of economic and social developments, people have organized intimate relationships and made choices that define their views of themselves and their places in society, in reliance on the availability of abortion in the event that contraception should fail. The ability of women to participate equally in the economic and social life of the nation has been facilitated by the ability to control their reproductive lives.

Christian Coalition believes that *Roe v. Wade* itself has created perhaps the gravest "profound and unnecessary damage to the Court's legitimacy" in our nation's history. That damage was merely compounded when the court elevated the expectations of some citizens regarding "the ability to control their reproductive lives" on a higher footing than the right to life of individual human beings.

Christian Coalition believes that ultimately there

should be a right-to-life statute or an amendment to the Constitution, to enshrine protection for unborn children and as a bulwark against other assaults on the right to life.

We hope to see a day when the Supreme Court abandons its pro-abortion ideology, recognizes the right to life of each human individual, and overturns its own erroneous rulings. We believe that the other, co-equal branches of government can and should responsibly challenge the Supreme Court to confront its profound errors regarding unborn children.

We cannot be content, however, merely to state these principles and then wait for political and social consensus to emerge to make them achievable. Respect for the sanctity of human life will continue to erode, unless we begin now to reverse governmental policies that, on an ever-expanding scale, promote abortion as routine "medical service," as a necessary method of birth control, as a source of tissue or organs for transplantation, or as a "cheap fix" for various social ills such as adolescent pregnancy.

Specifically, Christian Coalition is urging the current Congress to take the following concrete steps to curb government-sponsored promotion of abortion, and to begin the process of restoring respect for the sanctity of life of unborn children:

1. End taxpayer subsidies to organizations that promote and perform abortions.

Christian Coalition calls for an end to federal funding for programs and organizations that promote and perform abortions, both domestically and through the foreign aid program.

An obvious example, domestically, is Title X of the *Public Health Service Act*. This program currently consumes $193 million annually, most of which goes to some four thousand birth control clinics.

The Title X program was originally created in 1970, three years before *Roe v. Wade*, to provide "family planning" services to adults. The original Title X law provides that "none of the funds . . . shall be used in programs where abortion is a method of family planning."

However, in the ensuing years the program has become increasingly dominated by the Planned Parenthood Federation of America (PPFA), which operates the nation's largest chain of abortion clinics and gets an estimated $30 million to $40 million a year from the Title X program. The program has become overtly pro-abortion.

Presidents Reagan and Bush issued regulations to require clinics funded by Title X to stick to contraception and stop promoting abortion, but President Clinton wiped out those restrictions on his third day in office.

Under the current rules, all Title X-funded clinics are actually *required* to counsel every pregnant woman and girl who walks in the door regarding all of their "pregnancy management options," including "termination of pregnancy." In short, taxpayer money is being used to promote abortion essentially as simply an alternative method of birth control.

The Clinton rules also require the clinic staff, following such "counseling," to refer women and girls to abortion clinics when desired. Many of these abortion clinics are operated by the same organizations that operate the Title

X clinics (for example, a local Planned Parenthood affiliate). In practice, the government-funded clinics operate as funnels into the private abortion mills.

The Title X program is currently directed by Dr. Felicia Stewart, an obstetrician who previously worked as an abortionist for Planned Parenthood. Among her other qualifications, Stewart is the author of technical literature on the methodology of late-term abortions.

Even beyond the program's promotion of abortion, the merits of continued funding of Title X are highly questionable. It is estimated that one-third of the clients served through Title X funding are teenagers. Yet, during the twenty-five years that the program has existed at increasing funding levels, the out-of-wedlock pregnancy rate has doubled among girls fifteen to nineteen, the abortion rate among teens has also more than doubled, and sexually transmitted diseases among teens have increased sharply. Today, one out of every four sexually experienced teenagers becomes infected with a sexually transmitted disease annually.[7]

The administration's pro-abortion agenda is being pursued even more aggressively through the U.S. foreign aid program and through various UN agencies and conferences. During his presidential campaign, Bill Clinton had pledged to make abortions "rare." But as early as April 1, 1993, White House spokeswoman Dee Dee Myers said that the administration regarded abortion as "part of the overall approach to population control."[8] To direct the U.S. population control program, the President chose former U.S. Senator from Colorado, Tim Wirth, who now serves as Undersecretary of State for Global Affairs—only one notch under the Secretary of State.

Mr. Wirth further clarified the administration's doctrine in a speech to a UN population meeting on May 11, 1993, in which he said, "A government which is violating basic human rights should not hide behind the defense of sovereignty. . . . Our position is to support reproductive choice, including access to safe abortion."[9] Mr. Wirth also said a U.S. goal was to make such "reproductive choice" available to every woman by the year 2000.

To make legal abortion accessible to "all women" would require massive changes in the current abortion laws of less-developed nations. At least ninety-five nations have laws that are generally protective of pre-born human beings. In nearly all of Latin America, most of Africa, and much of the rest of the developing world, the laws generally protect the human fetus.

On March 16, 1994, the State Department sent an "action cable" to all overseas diplomatic and consular posts. The cable called for "senior level diplomatic interventions" with foreign governments in support of advancing U.S. population-control "priorities" at the then-approaching U.N.-sponsored world population conference in Cairo:

Posts [embassies] are requested to approach host governments to outline USG [U.S. government] negotiating priorities for the final preparatory committee meeting for the International Conference on Population and Development. . . . The priority issues for the U.S. include assuring . . . access to safe abortion. . . . The United States believes that access to safe, legal, and voluntary abortion is a fundamental right of all women. . . . The United States delegation will also be working for stronger language on the importance of access to abortion services.[10]

This cable, and the administration's "pro-abortion imperialism" in general, provoked many strongly negative responses both in the United States and from foreign governments. As a result, President Clinton, Vice President Gore, and Secretary of State Warren Christopher have adopted softer rhetorical tones—even giving lip service to the concept that each nation should be able to maintain the abortion laws that it desires.

But the policy thrust has not changed. Drawing on various foreign aid programs that now total at least $580 million annually, the administration is pumping massive amounts of U.S. taxpayer funds to organizations that are committed to the legalization of abortion throughout the world. For example, the administration has committed $75 million to the London headquarters of the International Planned Parenthood Federation (IPPF), which seeks to legalize abortion in less-developed nations.

Even more outrageous is the administration's restoration of funding to the United Nations Population Fund (UNFPA). The UNFPA is involved in a host of abortion-related activities, including funding of the French abortion pill (RU 486) for Third World women. In 1985, the Reagan administration determined that the UNFPA's extensive involvement in China's coercive population-control program violated a U.S. law, the Kemp Amendment, which prohibits funding to any organization that "supports or participates in the management of a program of coercive abortion or involuntary sterilization."

Even after the U.S. cutoff, China's program was repeatedly and vigorously defended by the UNFPA's top official, Executive Director Nafis Sadik, whose incredible pronouncements included these public statements: "The UNFPA firmly believes, and so does the government of the People's Republic of China, that their program is a totally voluntary program," and, "The implementation of the policy [in China] and the acceptance of the policy is purely voluntary."[11] The cutoff was challenged in court, but upheld in an opinion written by a liberal federal judge, Abner Mikva.[12]

Today, Abner Mikva serves as Counsel to the President —the chief White House lawyer. Nafis Sadik continues to direct the UNFPA, which remains heavily involved in China's population-control program. The Kemp Amendment is still the law—but the Clinton administration is funneling from $40 million to $50 million annually to the UNFPA.

Regarding China's program, Amnesty International USA recently outlined some of the reports coming out of China regarding a brutal birth control crackdown being conducted in Hebei Province under the slogan, "Better To Have More Graves Than More Than One Child":

[D]etainees were beaten and tortured to accelerate the payment of fines. Some were reportedly hung upside down, others received electric shocks on their tongue with electric batons or live wires. . . . One man who could not bear to see his wife tortured in a cell for days attempted to sell their children in Beijing . . . other women pregnant eight or nine months were given—against their will—injections to induce miscarriages.[13]

Of the millions of Chinese women and men brutalized by the one-child policy, a handful have made it to the United States. Under the Bush Administration, political asylum was granted to those few—no more than two hundred a year—who were able to demonstrate that they faced persecution because of their resistance to the one-child policy. The Clinton administration has reversed this policy, and is moving aggressively to deport even Chinese women who have already been subjected to compulsory abortions. Asked why, Undersecretary Wirth replied that if asylum were granted in such cases, "we could potentially open ourselves up to just about everybody in the world saying 'I don't want to plan my family, therefore I deserve political asylum.' "[14] The distinction between *voluntary* family planning and *government-coerced* sterilization and abortion is apparently of little consequence to Wirth.

Most Americans do not pay taxes for the purpose of empowering the U.S. government to export an abortion-on-demand ideology to nations whose peoples see the worth of unborn children more clearly than the majority of our Supreme Court justices. Nor, we believe, do they pay taxes with the idea of supporting a UN agency that whitewashes China's compulsory-abortion program. Christian Coalition calls on the 104th Congress to end funding for these programs.

2. Place real limits on abortions during the second-half of pregnancy.

It is an article of faith with many journalists and some politicians that a substantial majority of Americans are

74

firmly "pro-choice" on abortion. But a careful reading of public opinion polls reveals quite a different picture—and one considerably more hopeful to those who seek to protect unborn children.

For example, in February 1995, a *USA Today*–Gallup poll got this response from a scientifically chosen national sample:[15]

Do you think abortions should be . . .
Legal under any circumstances?	32%
Legal under most circumstances?	9%
Legal only in a few circumstances?	41%
Illegal in all circumstances?	15%
No opinion	3%

It is immediately evident that 56 percent—an absolute majority—said that abortion should be "legal in only a few circumstances" or "illegal in all circumstances." This is a far cry from the "pro-choice majority" so frequently invoked by media commentators.

When Americans are polled on the specific *circumstances* under which they believe abortion should be legal, the results are even more instructive. Various pollsters have found pluralities or narrow majorities in favor of limiting legal abortion to cases of danger to the life of the mother, rape, and incest. For example, a November 1994 poll by The Wirthlin Group found that 53 percent would allow abortion, at most, to save the life of the mother, or in rape, or incest cases.

In a 1991 Gallup poll, 73 percent of Americans said they "would support a prohibition of abortion after the first

75

three months of pregnancy, except where abortion is required to save the life of the mother."[16]

Indeed, most Americans believe that there are already stringent limits on abortion after the first three months of pregnancy—but they are misinformed. Currently, no state has meaningful restrictions on reasons for which abortions can be performed, or methods by which they can be performed, during second trimester of pregnancy. Many states have laws that attempt in some way to discourage abortions during the final three months of pregnancy—but most of these are so ridden with loopholes as to be little more than symbolic.

Some journalists and politicians often prefer to dismiss the subject of late-term abortions with the observation that "the great majority" of abortions occur during the first three months of pregnancy. That is true—but the absolute numbers of *reported* later abortions are frightful. There are about 168,000 abortions performed annually *after* the first three months of pregnancy. Of these, about 60,000 year are performed after sixteen weeks, and at least 11,000 after twenty weeks.[17]

Even though these numbers are staggering, they are surely much less than the actual numbers of late abortions performed. Reporting of abortions is largely voluntary, and there is evidence that very late abortions may be especially underreported. With modern neonatal assistance, babies born prematurely at around twenty-three weeks sometimes survive. By twenty-four weeks the survival rate is more than 50 percent at good neo-natal units, and it rises sharply after that point.

"Third trimester" abortions are those performed after

76

twenty-four weeks. When he served as Surgeon General, C. Everett Koop estimated that there are four thousand *third-trimester* abortions annually in the U.S.[18] Pro-abortion groups usually claim that there are at most a few hundred. A leading specialist in late-term abortions, asked by a medical newspaper to comment on this wide discrepancy, responded that "probably Koop's numbers are more correct."[19]

Most Americans would be shocked to learn about the methods that are used in late-term abortions in America today.

During the first decade after *Roe v. Wade,* there were frequent cases of babies being born alive during attempted late-term abortions. In 1981, the top abortion expert at the federal Centers for Disease Control estimated that four hundred to five hundred babies were being born alive in attempted abortions each year.[20] Most of these babies soon succumbed to their injuries and prematurity, but others survived; at least one is now a teenager active in the pro-life movement.[21]

The abortion industry responded by developing methods that were practically guaranteed to result in the death of the unborn child. This included refinement of a method called "dilation and extraction," or "D&E." In this method—used mainly during the fourth and fifth months of pregnancy—the abortionist dilates the cervix (the opening of the womb), inserts forceps and other instruments into the uterus, and pulls the baby apart by manual force.

One of the developers of this method, Dr. Warren Hern of Boulder, Colorado, commented:

Several authors agree that the D & E procedure is easier emotionally for the patient since she does not have to deliver a fetus which may have signs of life. . . . [However, S]ome part of our cultural and perhaps even biological heritage recoils at a destructive operation on a form that is similar to our own. . . . We have reached a point in this particular technology where there is no possibility of denial of an act of destruction by the operator. It is before one's eyes. The sensations of dismemberment flow through the forceps like an electric current.[22]

By about halfway through the pregnancy, however, this intrauterine dismemberment method becomes very difficult, due to the toughness of the baby's tissues and skeleton at this stage. For abortions done after this point—that is, after nineteen or twenty weeks—some abortionists have developed an alternative method—a method now referred to by various terms including "dilation and extraction," "cranial decompression," or "partial birth abortions."[23]

In a recent article on the partial birth method, Dr. Paul Ranalli, a professor of neurology at the University of Toronto, wrote:

It will be palpably obvious to anyone that such a procedure would be excruciatingly painful for anyone with the ability to feel pain. . . . Can the fetus at twenty-four weeks feel this procedure as we would? . . . [B]y the late second trimester, when the partial-birth procedure is [first] performed, the evidence is now quite convincing. The unavoidable truth is that our spino-thalamic (pain) system is established and fully connected by twenty to twenty-four weeks gestation. Elements of pain are probably felt by the fetus even earlier than this.[24]

Many partial birth abortions are performed even after the point of viability, when the babies could survive outside the womb with modern neonatal care. One specialist in partial birth abortions, Dr. James McMahon of Los Angeles, has said that he sometimes uses the procedure as late as forty weeks, which is full-term.[25]

Dr. McMahon admitted to ambivalence about what he does:

> I do have moral compunctions. And if I see a case that's later, like after twenty weeks where it frankly is a child to me, I really agonize over it . . . On the other hand, I have another position, which I think is superior in the hierarchy of questions, and that is, "Who owns the child?" It's got to be the mother.[26]

In 1993, the National Right to Life Committee disseminated about six million copies of a brochure describing the partial birth method. The booklet included a series of six drawings that accurately depicted the method, based on a technical paper in which Dr. Martin Haskell of Dayton, Ohio, explained in clinical detail how to perform the procedure.[27] In an interview with *American Medical News*, Dr. Haskell acknowledged that these drawings are accurate "from the technical point of view."[28]

The National Abortion Federation advised its members:

Don't apologize: this is a legal abortion procedure. . . . There are many reasons why women have
late abortions: life endangerment, fetal indications,
lack of money or health insurance, social-psychologi-
cal crises, lack of knowledge about human reproduc-
tion, etc.[29]

Those who hold the "don't apologize" view of partial
birth procedure will soon have an opportunity to make
their case before the Congress and the American people.
Congressman Charles Canady (R-Fla.), the chairman of
the Constitution Subcommittee of the U.S. House Judi-
ciary Committee, is preparing a bill to ban the use of the
partial birth abortion method nationwide.

Christian Coalition strongly supports Canady's proposal, both because it heightens public awareness of the
tragedy that has followed *Roe v. Wade,* and because the bill
could save thousands of infants from a having their lives
cut short in an especially horrible manner. Christian Coalition also supports additional well-crafted legislation to
prevent all late-term abortions.

In supporting Canady's bill we are steadfast in maintaining that all innocent human life deserves legal and
constitutional protection. We remain dedicated to working
toward the day when every child is safe in its mother's
womb.

3. Protect the rights of states that do not wish to use taxpayer funds to take innocent life.

Christian Coalition believes taxpayer funds should only be used to pay for an abortion when the mother's life is in danger.

After the Supreme Court legalized abortion in 1973, the federal government began paying for elective abortions through Medicaid, a program through which the federal and state governments jointly provide medical benefits for eligible low-income Americans. By 1976, the program was paying for nearly three hundred thousand elective abortions per year.

In 1976, however, a freshman Republican congressman from Illinois, Henry J. Hyde, succeeded in enacting an amendment that prohibited federal funding of abortion "except where the life of the mother would be endangered if the fetus were carried to term." The Hyde Amendment reduced the number of federally funded abortions from 300,000 a year to around 200.

In the absence of government-subsidized abortions, many low-income women obtained abortions paid for from other sources—but an estimated 20 percent did not. Thus, by the time Bill Clinton was elected president in 1992, perhaps one million children were alive because of Congressman Hyde's amendment.

During the Bush Administration, Congress passed several bills to weaken the Hyde Amendment and several similar laws, but these bills were all vetoed by President Bush. The situation changed drastically with the election of Bill Clinton in November, 1992. President Clinton took

81

office carrying a long list of promises made to pro-abortion advocacy groups during his presidential campaign—including repeal of the Hyde Amendment.

Pro-life lobbyists determined that there were insufficient votes in the House and the Senate to renew the traditional Hyde Amendment language.

Faced with the disastrous prospect of Congress repealing the Hyde Amendment and restoring tax-funded abortion on demand,[30] Congressman Hyde made a difficult decision: he reintroduced his amendment, permitting federal funding of abortions in cases of rape and incest (in addition to the life-of-mother exception). Mr. Hyde's move caught the pro-abortion forces off guard, and swung a large bloc of swing votes into Mr. Hyde's corner. Confounding the pundits, the House adopted the revised Hyde Amendment by a fifty-four-vote margin.

Mr. Hyde's victory—later ratified by the Senate—dissipated much of the political momentum that the pro-abortion forces had carried out of the 1992 election, and substantially disrupted the entire pro-abortion legislative agenda for the rest of the 1993–94 Congress. The resounding renewal of the Hyde Amendment spelled the death-knell for the *Freedom of Choice Act*, a bill to prohibit states from placing even the most minimal restrictions on abortion, such as a twenty-four-hour waiting period or parental consent laws.

Congressman Hyde said that the intent of his revised amendment was to *allow* states to obtain partial reimbursement from the federal government for abortions provided in cases of rape and incest—but not to *mandate* that any state provide such abortions. Nevertheless, in December 1993, senior Clinton administration officials—ignoring earlier promises to respect "state flexibility" regarding state abortion-funding policies—sent out the first in a series of directives, *mandating* that each state begin providing abortions in cases of rape and incest.

The administration's directives opened the door to a blizzard of legal attacks on states that had policies of using tax funding of abortion only to save the mother's life. By early 1995, the majority of such states had reluctantly complied with the administration decrees, but at least seven were still resisting; administration officials were threatening to cut off all Medicaid funds to these recalcitrant states.

In Colorado and Arkansas, voters had in earlier years approved amendments to their state constitutions, prohibiting state funding of abortion. In 1994, federal judges ruled that the new federal policy created "conflicts" with these state laws. These judges resolved these "conflicts" by totally invalidating these pro-life constitutional amendments, opening the door to state-funded abortion on demand in these states. In 1995, a federal judge in North Dakota issued a similar ruling.

Pro-lifers in Arkansas saw a bitter irony in the invalidation of their pro-life constitutional amendment. When that amendment had first been proposed in 1986, Governor Bill Clinton had sent a letter to Arkansas Right to Life in which he said:

I am opposed to abortion and to government funding of abortions. We should not spend state funds on abortions because so many people believe abortion is wrong. I do support the concept of the proposed Arkansas Constitutional Amendment 65 and agree with its stated purpose.[31]

The amendment permitted state-funded abortions only to save the life of the mother. In early 1995, Congressman Ernest Istook (D-Okla.) proposed an amendment to restore authority to each state to decide whether or not to pay for abortions (except for life-of-mother abortions, which would remain federally mandated). For pro-lifers, insult was added to injury when President Clinton's chief spokesman, Michael McCurry, said that the Istook Amendment was the product of "extremists in the Right to Life movement" and "beyond outrageous."[32]

In fact, however, the Istook Amendment would do nothing more than restore the policy endorsed by Governor Clinton in 1986. If the policy favored by Governor Clinton in 1986 is to be regarded as "extremist," the question arises of when Mr. Clinton ceased being an extremist.

Christian Coalition urges that the 104th Congress promptly enact the Istook Amendment in order to permit states to prohibit tax funding of non-lifesaving abortions. Senator James Exon (D-Neb.) has introduced a similar amendment in the Senate.

7

Encouraging Support
of Private Charities

*Enactment of legislation to enhance contributions to private
charities as a first step toward transforming the bureaucratic
welfare state into a system of private and
faith-based compassion.*

A 1994 REPORT by the National Center for Policy Analysis
details the growing evidence that private sector charities
do a better job than government of "getting prompt aid to
those who need it most, encouraging self-sufficiency and
self-reliance, preserving the family unit and using resources [more] efficiently."[1]

At the same time, it is clear that America's welfare system is a tragic failure. Despite record expenditures, poverty is getting worse, not better. Indeed, the current
welfare system is actually contributing to poverty in
America.

Federal, state, and local governments spend about $350
billion per year on seventy-nine means-tested programs
aimed at assisting the poor; this is about 20 percent more

85

than we spend on national defense. Yet today's poverty rate of 15.1 percent is higher than the 14.7 percent rate in 1966 when the War on Poverty began.

Even worse, the welfare system has caused the work ethic of the lowest income groups to collapse and family breakup and illegitimacy to soar. In 1960, nearly two-thirds of households in the lowest one-fifth of the income distribution were headed by persons who worked. By 1991, this had declined to around one-third, with only 11 percent of the heads of households working full-time, year-round. And then there are the statistics on illegitimacy. The rate for African-Americans has risen from 28 percent in 1965 to 68 percent in 1991. The rate for whites was 4 percent in 1965, and among white high school dropouts it is now 48 percent. In ten major U.S. cities in 1991, more than half of all births occur out of wedlock.

The collapse of work and family has bred urban decay, crime, drug addiction, and numerous other social afflictions. This social tragedy is the direct result of our current welfare system which rewards people for not working by giving them numerous benefits and penalizes those who return to work by taking away the benefits. The system rewards illegitimacy and family breakup by paying women generous rewards for having children while they are single and penalizes marriage by taking away the benefits from women who marry working men.

Simply stated, the current welfare system is a disaster for the poor, the taxpayers, the economy, and the nation. Even more importantly, our current welfare system stands in direct contradiction to one of history's lessons about helping the poor: Private charity works better than government handouts. Christian Coalition believes that the time has come to remember our history lessons and begin to move back to a system of private charity.

A New Approach to Welfare

One way to accomplish this would be to abolish all major federal welfare programs and give the money to the states in the form of block grants. States could then use those dollars to involve private and religious charitable organizations.

Another possibility is to give taxpayers the ability to "target" their welfare tax dollars to private charitable organizations *or* the government. Both ideas are worth pursuing.

Federal funding for as many current federal welfare programs as possible should be sent to the states with only one proviso: that the funds be used to help the poor. Each state would then be able to use the funds, along with current state welfare funds, to design its own welfare programs. These grants would replace AFDC, food stamps, and public housing, among other so-called entitlement programs. Medicaid funds could be segregated in a separate grant with the requirement that they be spent on health care for the poor.

This would free each state to experiment with entirely new approaches to welfare. States might offer work instead of welfare. They might grant funds to well-run private charities. They might come up with entirely new approaches that no one has thought of yet.

The federal government should not impede innovation and experimentation at the state level. Clearly the federal government does not know what the right approach to welfare is, and the right approach may vary from state to state. Moreover, any attempt to impose federal restrictions on the design of state welfare programs will tend to give Washington-based interest groups greater opportunity to influence policy and short circuit fundamental reforms. With open experimentation, by contrast, some states will be able to discover what works, and others can adopt and adapt the best approaches.

Increasing Credit for Charitable Contributions

The second possibility for reform would be a dollar-for-dollar tax credit for contributions to private charities. Taxpayers could donate a percentage of their personal income tax payments, perhaps the share of total individual income taxes that currently goes to federal means-tested welfare programs. To the extent that a state's taxpayers utilized such credits, the state's welfare block grants would be reduced by an equal amount. Thus the revenue loss from the tax credits would be offset completely by reduced federal welfare grants to the states, leaving no effect on the deficit. Block grants plus tax credits would give taxpayers the ultimate control over welfare. If a state misspent its block grant funds, its taxpayers could shift the funds to the private alternatives that work better. Healthy market competition between the state programs and private charities would give state welfare bureaucracies a real incentive to perform well in reducing poverty.

A mountain of evidence and experience indicates that private charities are far more effective than public welfare bureaucracies. Studies show, for example, that "as many as 80 percent of low-income people turn to the private sector first when facing a crisis."[2] Private agencies engaged in job training for teenagers and for the mentally and physically handicapped have shown they can out-perform government agencies. Instead of encouraging counterproductive behavior, the best private charities use their aid to encourage self-improvement, self-sufficiency, and ultimate independence. The assistance of private charities may be contingent on ending drug use and alcoholism, completing necessary education, taking available work, avoiding out-of-wedlock births, maintaining families, and other positive behaviors.[3] Private charities are also much better at getting aid promptly to those who need it most and at getting the most benefit out of every dollar.

With the tax credit, private organizations would be able to compete on a level playing field for welfare tax dollars. To the extent they convinced the taxpayers that they were doing a better job than state bureaucracies, private charities, rather than government, would be permitted to manage America's war on poverty.

Private Charities Are Efficient

Although volumes have been written about the failures of government welfare programs, the academic and scholarly community has paid surprisingly little attention to private sector charity. Yet the private sector is playing an extremely important role: In 1992, total charitable contributions reached $124 billion, with contributions by individuals accounting for 82 percent ($101.83 billion) of that total.

More than 85 percent of adult Americans make some charitable contribution each year. About half the adult population did volunteer work in 1991, contributing more than twenty billion hours of labor. The dollar value of these contributions of time is at least $176 billion. If the value of volunteer labor is included, private sector contributions to charitable causes are approximately the same as the poverty budgets of federal, state, and local governments combined.

Many citizens are not as generous in their contributions to private charitable organizations these days because they already are overtaxed. However, if given the choice between having their tax dollars subsidize government welfare programs or subsidize private charitable programs, many would prefer to designate the money to a private charity of their choice.

The reasons for this are several. Entitlement programs for welfare are so structured, for example, that benefits are granted solely on the basis of personal circumstances. Applicants do not have to give the reasons for their circumstances or explain how they plan to change them in the future. They do not even have to show a willingness to change. In the AFDC program, the requirements for eligibility essentially amount to: (1) low income, (2) very few assets, (3) dependent children, and (4) no man in the household. Anyone satisfying these requirements is entitled to benefits. And the word *entitlement* means *right*—benefits cannot be withdrawn simply because recipients refuse to modify their behavior.

The philosophy of the private sector is quite different. The best private charities do not view the giving of assistance as a "duty" or the receipt of assistance as a "right." Instead, they view charitable assistance as a tool recipients can use intelligently, not only to gain relief but also to change behavior. At many private charities the level of assistance varies considerably from individual to individual. Private agencies usually reserve the right to reduce assistance or withdraw it altogether if recipients do not make behavioral changes.

Many private charities require that a caseworker and an aid recipient develop a plan to move the recipient into self-sufficiency. For example:

• At Jessie's House, a transitional home for the homeless in Hampton, Massachusetts, shelter beyond one week is contingent upon evidence of individual improvement.

• At the Dallas Salvation Army, aid varies according to the caseworker's evaluation of the recipient's condition and record of behavioral improvement.

In contrast, entitlement programs grant recipients and potential recipients of aid broad freedoms to exercise their preferences. In many cases, they choose poverty and, in effect, present the rest of us with a welfare bill. The preferences of public welfare recipients thereby determine the behavior of those who pay the bills.

The philosophy of the private sector is quite different. In general, private agencies allow those who pay the bills to set the standards. Recipients of private sector welfare must adjust their behavior to the preferences of the rest of society, not the other way around.

If we accept the view that individuals should take responsibility for supporting themselves and their families and that welfare assistance should be administered in a way that encourages this behavior, it follows that the approach of our best private charities is far superior to that of entitlement programs. Because individuals and individual circumstances differ, it is only through hands-on management that we can give relief without encouraging antisocial behavior.

Hands-on management includes the tailoring of aid to individual needs and individual circumstances. Such support, counseling, and follow-up is virtually unheard of in federal welfare programs. Indeed, when public welfare recipients request counseling, they frequently are referred to private sector agencies.

A basic premise of the American system is that government is the last resort. In other words, the role of government is to do those socially desirable things that the private sector either will not or cannot do.

Ironically, in the field of social welfare this premise has been turned on its head. In the early years of the War on Poverty, federal welfare programs were a social safety net to provide services that the private sector, for one reason or another, did not. Now it is obvious that just the opposite is true—increasingly, the private sector reaches people government does not reach and offers essential services that government welfare programs do not provide.

Failing Those with the Greatest Need

If a humane welfare system means anything at all, it means getting aid first to people who need it most. One of the most astonishing and least-known facts about the welfare state is how miserably it fails to achieve this goal. Consider that only 41 percent of all poverty families receive food stamps; yet 28 percent of food stamp families have incomes above the poverty level. Only 23 percent of all poverty families live in public housing or receive housing subsidies; yet almost half of the families receiving housing benefits are not poor. Only 40 percent of all poverty families are covered by Medicaid; yet 40 percent of all Medicaid beneficiaries are not poor. Amazingly, 41 percent of all poverty families receive no means-tested benefit of any kind from government; yet more than half of all families who do receive at least one means-tested benefit are not poor.

Where do people in need turn for help when they are not getting government assistance? They turn to private charities. Ninety-four percent of all shelters for the homeless in the U.S. are operated by churches, synagogues, secular groups, and other voluntary organizations.[4]

Our best private charities see independence and self-sufficiency as a primary goal for their "clients." Often this goal is accomplished by either encouraging or requiring aid recipients to contribute their labor to the agency itself.

But a major issue in the welfare–poverty industry is whether the recipient of aid should have to "do anything" in order to continue receiving welfare benefits. Nowhere is the controversy more evident than with respect to workfare.

Throughout the 1970s, a continuous political battle at the national level raged over the question of whether welfare should be tied to work. It appeared the welfare bureaucracy lost the battle when Congress passed the Work Incentive (WIN) program and the Community Work Experience Program (CWEP). However, because it administers these two programs, the bureaucracy that lost the battle won the war by finding few AFDC recipients suitable for workfare and channeling those who were suitable into training or school rather than jobs. The 1988 *Federal Family Support Act* mandated that all states create work-for-welfare programs. But as happened with WIN and CWEP, this program did not reduce the welfare rolls significantly.

Encouraging Compassion and Responsibility

A prevalent philosophy in the private sector is that most people are fully capable of taking responsibility for their lives in the long term, but that emergencies and crises occur for which help is both necessary and desirable. As a consequence, private sector agencies make it surprisingly easy for recipients to obtain emergency relief. It really is true that, in America, almost anybody can get a free lunch.

The near-universal characteristic of private sector charity is that it's easy to get, but hard to keep. Most government programs, by contrast, have the opposite characteristic: it's hard to get on welfare, but easy to stay there. In the public sector, there are often long waiting times between applying for assistance and receiving aid. In Texas, for example, the waiting period is typically two to three weeks for food stamps. For AFDC, the waiting period is typically a month after an applicant completes the complicated and cumbersome application forms.

Once accepted into the public welfare system, however, people find it relatively easy to stay there for a long time: Of all women who receive welfare in any given year, about 60 percent receive welfare the next year. Among women receiving welfare for two consecutive years, about 70 percent receive it a third year. Among women receiving welfare for four consecutive years, about 80 percent receive it a fifth year.

There is considerable evidence that private sector charity makes far more efficient use of resources than do public welfare programs. Although temporary relief in the form of food or shelter is fairly easy to obtain from private agencies, long-term assistance or assistance in the form of cash is far more difficult. For example, before the Dallas Salvation Army will provide cash to help people defray the cost of rent, recipients must present a court ordered eviction notice showing failure to pay rent.

Similarly, before that charity will give financial aid to defray the costs of utilities, the recipient must present a notice of termination of service for failure to pay utility bills. Even when there is evidence of need, good private charities often seek to determine whether the potential recipient has access to other, untapped sources of assistance. For example, before the Dallas Salvation Army will provide continuing assistance to an individual, a caseworker informs the family including in-laws and requests assistance from them first. The caseworker also makes sure the individual applies for all other public and private aid for which he or she is eligible.

Private sector agencies appear to be much more adept at avoiding unnecessary spending that does not benefit the truly needy. They know how to keep program costs down by utilizing volunteer labor and donated goods. Public housing placed in the hands of tenants costs less and is of higher quality than that owned and maintained by government. Private sector crime prevention programs, alcohol and drug abuse programs, and neighborhood preservation programs also have proved to be superior to public sector programs.

All of this supports one very important reality. In the words of Acton Institute head Father Robert A. Sirico,

"[G]overnment has no monopoly on compassion. Indeed, government is compassion's least able practitioner." Christian Coalition supports finding ways to ensure that the private sector is able to reassert itself as the rightful practitioner of charity to America's most needy.

8

Restricting Pornography

Protecting children from exposure to pornography on the Internet and cable television, and from sexual exploitation by child pornographers.

PORNOGRAPHY, BOTH SOFT-CORE AND HARD-CORE, is freely available on the Internet to virtually anyone with a home computer. Several magazines post pornographic images that can be viewed by anyone, including children, for free. There are also numerous sites on the Internet where hard-core pornography depicting a variety of explicit sexual acts, even rape scenes and bestiality, are available free and can be accessed with a few clicks of a computer button.

About a decade ago, pornography and the harm left in its wake were topics of intense discussions. It was during that period of time that the most comprehensive study of pornography, the Attorney General's Commission on Pornography, also known as the Meese Commission, came forth with its findings about pornography's victims—children, women, men, and families. Since that time, however, the face and the marketing of pornography have changed. Pornography that was once low-quality material sold in seedy, out-of-the-way stores is now being main-streamed in attractive packaging for sale in neighborhoods.

If new computer technologies have expanded opportunities for people to interact with one another, pursue their interests, and gather knowledge, they are also opening new avenues for traffic in pornography and other sexually explicit material. On the Internet, there are countless news groups centered on sex. Some of the best-selling CDs—compact disks for computers—are high-tech offerings of the kind of material seen in *Penthouse* and *Playboy* magazines. Seemingly every cable system has channels featuring soft-core and hard-core pornography. At a time when Americans are increasingly aware of the breakdown of values in our society and the urgency of restoring them, Congress should take steps to limit the spread of pornography over the information highway and elsewhere, especially with regard to children.

If adults are allowed a wide berth in the kind of materials they produce and disseminate in a free society, that latitude at the very least should not extend to exploiting children or polluting their minds. A tragedy in American society today is how soon it robs children of their innocence, a priceless commodity that can never be regained once lost. Christian Coalition supports three simple reforms: enactment of legislation to protect children from being exposed to pornography on the Internet; legislation to require cable television companies to completely block the video and audio on pornography channels to non-subscribers; and, amending the federal child pornography law to make it illegal to possess any child pornography.

Pornographers Invade the Internet

It didn't take long for the information superhighway, the tangle of computer and phone connections running around the world, to become a popular byway for pornographers and the sexually licentious. Without having to leave their home, people can solicit sex, download pornographic material, or send their own material around the world. According to *Newsweek*,[1] the second largest computer bulletin board in the country is called KinkNet. It features personal ads and special groups for sado-masochists and homosexuals. Members of the bulletin board can hold on-line orgies, typing out their sexual acts as they go. Another network in New York called "Electric Eye" has picture files organized into categories such as "Women in Bondage" and "Women Who Love Women." Other on-line services offer interactive erotic games. *Playboy* and *Penthouse* have their own locations where they hawk their various wares. So pervasive is cyber-porn that officials at the Lawrence Livermore nuclear weapons laboratory near San Francisco revealed last July that the lab's computers had been used by computer hackers to store and distribute more than one thousand hard-core pornographic images.[2]

The anonymity of the Internet leads to many of its more disturbing abuses. People who once would have kept their unnatural urges to themselves can find support in cyberspace. One newsgroup on Usenet has a name beginning "alt.sex.pedophile." According to the *Wall Street Journal* it contains digitized photos with titles such as "Girls at Play" and "Boys." Another newsgroup named "alt.sex.intergen" has users who trade impassioned defenses of pedophilia.[3] Because it provides a forum for talking anonymously, the Internet has become a favorite cruising spot of would-be molesters. Police investigators posing on the Internet as young computer nerds will get lewd solicitations from grown men trying to establish a relationship. "You just shake your head and wonder how many of these people are out there," one investigator told the *Miami Herald*.[4] The information highway clearly has seedy byways.

And frequently, the harm does not end at the computer terminal. There are numerous documented cases where individuals with a history of child exploitation and molestation have used computer bulletin boards to contact children, learn their names and addresses, and set up meetings with them. "We've already had rapes of children occur through that type of setup," says antipornography activist Len Munsil.[5]

Compact discs are being exploited in similar ways as the computer networks. One popular disk allows users to attempt to entice women into bed. Providing the wrong lines for the male character in the story will get him slapped in the face or otherwise rejected. The right lines mean the character gets sex, which the user then watches on the computer screen.[6] The best-selling pornographic CD-ROM is called "Virtual Valerie." It features a 3-D fantasy woman that the user tries to arouse, with a meter on the screen keeping track of the results. Most of the pornographic CD-ROMs similarly conceive of sex as a game, with the object being to "score" as much as possible.[7]

In the case of the Internet, similarly pornographic material is readily available to children. No longer is pornography behind a store counter where there are barriers to minors; it is potentially available on a home computer screen with just the right computer software and a few clicks of the mouse.

Parents should not have to worry about their children spending time on the computer. It should be something they encourage. But it cannot be as long as the Internet is crawling with easily accessible pornography. The current state of the Internet and the laws governing it risk changing the standard of decency in American society; materials once considered inappropriate to put in the hands of children now can get there with ease.

Congress can take a couple of steps to prevent new technologies from effecting this disturbing change by default. First, it should clarify the criminal code to include computers in the ban on transmitting obscene materials by a facility of interstate commerce. Computers are likely covered already by this law, but making it explicit will avoid possible misinterpretations by the courts and settle the matter with finality. This will make it clear that hardcore pornography—obscenity—is illegal on the information superhighway. It doesn't, however, address soft-core pornography such as pictures from *Playboy*. As its second step, therefore, Congress should amend the criminal code to make it illegal to transmit material harmful to minors, such as soft-core pornography, with reckless disregard of whether children will come into its possession. This will bring the same standard that prevents a convenience store clerk from selling children pornographic magazines to the Internet. These reforms will keep the new technologies from becoming ways to subvert old, indispensible standards.

Restricting Access to Adult Cable Channels

Cable television systems should get the same treatment. If you're not a subscriber it's nearly impossible to pick up channels like Disney or HBO; they're blocked out by the cable system. And for good reason. Why pay to subscribe to these channels if you can get them for free? But this logic doesn't seem always to apply to channels offering pornography. Sometimes the audio from these channels is left unblocked, meaning the channel surfer will hear lewd language and obscene sounds. Or the video may be incompletely blocked, leaving flickering images for any viewer to see. Needless to say, children will be among the stray viewers. Last year the American Family Association distributed to Congress a videotape of a pornographic channel that was transmitting its programming almost entirely unscrambled into the homes of nonsubscribers. And the channel was between two children's channels. Congress should pass a criminal statute to require cable companies to block pornographic channels entirely. Pornographic programming simply should not be allowed to be pumped indiscriminately into the homes of American families.

Loopholes in Child Pornography Laws

Few in society are tolerant of child pornography. It was viewed as a great surprise, therefore, when the Clinton administration found itself arguing on behalf of a man being prosecuted for child pornography infractions.

In 1991, Stephen Knox found himself the object of Justice Department prosecution after it was discovered that he had three videotapes showing partially clad prepubescent girls in sexually suggestive poses. He was initially convicted and sentenced to five years in prison. His appeal was based on an argument that the tapes were not actually child pornography because the girls were partially clothed and none of their genitalia were visible.

The Bush adminstration argued against Knox, but under President Clinton and Janet Reno at the Justice Department, the U.S. government helped Knox win a round in court last year. Although an outraged U.S. Senate unanimously passed an amendment disagreeing with the Justice Department's position, and although a federal appeals court eventually upheld Knox's original conviction, there is a lot of concern about the message that the administration and the case sent. And there is a renewed fear that the Knox case could result in the expansion of child pornography.

As a further step to protect children, Christian Coalition believes Congress should close a glaring loophole in the nation's child pornography laws. In 1988, President Reagan attempted to get legislation passed that would have made it illegal to possess any pieces of child pornography. The hope was the new law would prompt persons who had collections of child pornography to destroy them for fear of being prosecuted. But in an eleventh-hour compromise the bill was changed. In a conference committee of members of the House and Senate, they changed the Reagan language to criminalize only the possession of three or more items of child pornography such as pictures, magazines, videos, and so on. Thus, federal law sanctions the possession of some child pornography, as long as it is less than three pieces. A person with two hour-long videotapes depicting the rape of a child cannot be charged with a federal crime while someone with three photos depicting a child in a lascivious pose can. This sort of distinction is obviously nefarious and undercuts the rationale of the entire law. *Any* child pornography is a repugnant exploitation of children and should be treated as contraband. Congress should move to amend the child pornography law to make any possession illegal.

Making these reforms will help Congress help families protect their children from foul influences in American society. Too often we think that it is the responsibility of families to guard children from seeing or hearing inappropriate things. To a large extent it is. But that doesn't mean society should not work to minimize the number of dangers families have to protect against. If the broader society is constantly bombarding families with sexually suggestive or outright obscene messages, more and more of them will slip through, no matter how strong a family's defenses. Congress should come to the aid of families as advances in communications technology leads to a proliferation in the ways inappropriate materials can be disseminated.

It matters deeply what our children see and read. It shapes the landscape of their psyches. Hearing the unthinkable makes it thinkable. Seeing women in degrading situations lessens the way we think of them. Every piece of pornography tears a little hole in our society's soul—in the way we think of ourselves and of others. This is a truth that has been recognized over the centuries in almost every society. And for good measure the Meese Commission in the 1980s largely confirmed it. It is time we started acting on this common sense. If reading Shakespeare is uplifting, then exposure to obscenity is demeaning. Ensuring that children cannot do the latter is just as important as getting them to do the former.

9

Privatizing the Arts

The National Endowment for the Arts, National Endowment for the Humanities, Corporation for Public Broadcasting, and Legal Services Corporation should become voluntary organizations funded through private contributions.

CHRISTIAN COALITION URGES the privatization of the National Endowment for the Arts (NEA) because we do not view such funding as a proper role for the United States Government. The issue is not *whether* the arts should receive funding, but rather *which* entity should give funding —the government or the private sector.

Through its grant selection process, the NEA acts as an arbiter of art and places its endorsement or seal of approval on certain works. According to *The New York Times*, officials at the endowment say their grants serve as an imprimatur, a seal of approval, making it easier for artists and arts groups to raise money from other sources.[1] This federal imprimatur is as important to artists as is the funding which accompanies the grant.

And yet, as former Secretary of Education William Bennett pointed out during his testimony calling for elimination of the NEA, this role of arbiter itself should be questioned, as well as the seal of approval which gives the official blessing—the blessing of the people of the United States—to things both worthy and horrible.[2]

As Bennett pointed out, artists and academics, to say nothing of civil libertarians, should all be made profoundly uneasy by the federal government performing such a role of arbiter through its underwriting of various projects. The federal government's endorsement of projects is particularly objectionable when it applies to obscenity, pornography, or attacks on religion.

Despite repeated attempts by the United States Congress to place common-sense restrictions on federal funding of the arts, NEA dollars continue to go toward controversial works that denigrate the religious beliefs and moral values of mainstream Americans.[3] William Donohue, president of the Catholic League for Religious and Civil Rights, has joined the call for eliminating funding for the NEA, stating, "We, as Catholics, have rights too, and among them is the right not to be defamed, and this is especially true when defamation is funded with government money."

It has become clear that the United States Congress has been able to exert very little control over the agency. Based on the NEA's past history, any attempts to place congressional restrictions on its use of taxpayer dollars will either be overruled by the courts or ignored by the agency.

Public Funding for Obscene Art

Over the years, the NEA has incurred the anger of individual members of Congress, but it was not until 1989 that the agency became the focus of intense criticism. The 1989 controversy was sparked by two NEA-funded exhibits which many found offensive. The Andres Serrano series, which was subsidized by $15,000 of NEA funding, offended many Christians with its "Piss Christ," a photograph of a crucifix immersed in the artist's urine, as well as its other works, such as "Piss Pope" and "Piss God." The Robert Mapplethorpe exhibit, funded with $30,000 of NEA funds, contained nude photographs of children and explicit homoerotic photography.

As a result of the uproar which developed over these works, the United States Congress placed restrictions on the use of NEA funds, "explicitly prohibiting the use of funds to promote, disseminate, or produce materials which in the judgment of the National Endowment for the Arts . . . may be considered obscene, including but not limited to, depictions of sadomasochism, homoeroticism, the sexual exploitation of children, or individuals engaged in sex acts and which, when taken as a whole, do not have serious literary, artistic, political, or scientific value." One might have thought that the addition of this legislative language would have resolved the issue, but that was not the case.

In order to comply with this congressional mandate, the NEA began requiring artists to sign statements indicating their willingness to comply with the restriction. Several of the grantees balked at this requirement, refused to sign the required certifications, and brought suit in federal court challenging the constitutionality of the practice. A California federal district court sided with the artists and held that the certification requirement was unconstitutionally vague since the NEA determined what constituted obscenity, and it infringed on the artists' speech rights. The NEA dropped the certification requirement shortly thereafter.

In the meantime, during 1990, the U.S. Congress had reauthorized the NEA and enacted its fiscal year 1991 appropriations bill. The final version of the legislation dropped the 1989 obscenity ban, and instead required the chairperson to consider general standards of decency and respect for the diverse beliefs and values of the American public in awarding NEA grants. It left the determination of whether funded projects were obscene to the courts, and authorized the NEA to obtain subsequent reimbursement for the funding spent on obscene work before additional funding would be granted to an artist.

Nevertheless, in December 1990, NEA Chairman John Frohnmayer announced that he would not deny any grants for projects violating the decency clause. In addition, the decency restriction was also challenged in court and held to be unconstitutionally vague and violative of the artists' rights to speech and artistic expression.[4] A clear pattern emerged of the thwarting of congressional intent by agency officials and the courts. Public criticism of the agency continued as controversial artists and organizations continued to receive NEA funding. Efforts continued in 1991 and 1993 to reduce or eliminate the agency's funding through amendments on the House floor.

But despite having been afforded the opportunity, the NEA has consistently resisted efforts to get its affairs in order. The latest example is Ron Athey's performance at Minneapolis's Walker Art Center in March of 1994. This federally-subsidized performance consisted of Mr. Athey carving a design in an assistant's back, dabbing the blood onto paper towels, and then sending the towels on a clothesline out over the shocked audience. Jane Alexander, the NEA chairwoman, defended the work. *The Washington Post* quoted Alexander as stating that "[n]ot all art is for everybody, and that Americans are certainly not used to seeing bloodletting, except in films, and when it happens in person it must be surprising."

However, the United States Congress did see something wrong with this use of tax dollars. It rebuked the NEA last year by reducing its funding by two percent due to this performance. Yet, as noted above, NEA Chairwoman Jane Alexander saw nothing wrong with it, and the NEA has once again awarded federal funding to the Walker Art Center.

Unfortunately, the examples of bigotry funded through taxpayer dollars over the years are not isolated. Cardinal John O'Connor was described as that "creep in black skirts" in a catalog for an exhibit funded with the help of NEA dollars.[5] "Christ uttered obscenities and condoned all types of sexual activity as consistent with biblical teaching" another NEA-funded production asserted.[6]

It has been pointed out that all too often government funding supports artists who seem less interested in creating art or fostering knowledge and more interest in ridiculing, provoking, and antagonizing mainstream American values.[7]

At a time of fiscal restraint and budget austerity, cultural agencies cannot expect to be exempt from the broader realities of declining federal spending. Americans spend more than $7 billion annually on the arts; only $173 million is derived from federal funding. The privatization of the NEA into a voluntary, charitable organization would unleash the creative capacity of the American people and depoliticize one of the most controversial agencies in recent years. It is an idea whose time has come.

Politicizing the Humanities

The National Endowment for the Humanities (NEH) also would be improved by privatization. Lynne Cheney, the NEH chairwoman from 1986 to 1992, testified in January in support of ending federal funding for the agency. During her testimony she explained how the humanities —like the arts—have become highly politicized. Many academics and artists now see their purpose not as revealing truth or beauty, but as achieving social and political transformation. Government should not be funding those whose main interest is promoting an agenda.[8] The controversial national history standards, which NEH funding assisted in bringing into existence, are one such example.

William Bennett, also a former chairman of the National Endowment for the Humanities, similarly testified to this politicization. He cited as an example his efforts at the NEH to institute a summer literary program for high school teachers. The purpose of the program was to provide an opportunity for teachers to study in depth a classical literary work, whether it be in philosophy, literature, or history. However, he found that by the third year of the program's existence, "[t]he books were being Marxized, feminized, deconstructed, and politicized, and the teachers were being indoctrinated in the prevailing dogmas of academia."[9]

Despite her efforts while chairwoman to ameliorate this politicization, Lynne Cheney has now concluded that the

110

federal subsidization of the Endowment should be eliminated. She explained:

> Government should not be funding those whose main interest is promoting an agenda. . . . I remember one film project that used a most decided double standard to judge Western civilization. It declared Christopher Columbus guilty of "genocide," while portraying the Aztecs, who practiced human sacrifice on a massive scale, as a gentle, peace-loving people. When I vetoed this project, the historical establishment rose up to denounce me roundly for, ironically enough, "politicizing the NEH"—but, in fact, I had done what the taxpayers had hired me to do—[keep] their money from being used to promote a political viewpoint. It is impossible, however, given the current state of the arts and humanities, always to be successful at this effort.[10]

Supporters of the arts and humanities cannot expect the general public to provide funding for the arts and humanities through tax dollars, and yet not object when the projects funded offend their moral sensibilities.

The NEH's funding of the Modern Language Association is yet another example of the agency's use of taxpayer dollars. According to Bennett: "[T]he NEH provides funding for the Modern Language Association (MLA). . . . Their annual convention attracts over 10,000 professors and students and reveals the type of agenda that NEH grants make possible. Past panels include such topics as 'Lesbian Tongues United'; 'Henry James and Queer Performativity;' [and] 'Status of Gender and Feminism in

111

Queer Theory.' "[11] It is clear that at a time when more than 24 percent of the American family's budget goes to the federal government in taxes, we can find a better use for these tax dollars than through continued funding of the NEH. The arts and humanities were flourishing in our country long before the establishment of the Endowments thirty years ago, and will continue to do so independent of federal funding to these agencies.

Why PBS Doesn't Need a Government Check

The Corporation for Public Broadcasting (CPB) is another entity that should rely on private funding. Federal subsidies to the Public Broadcasting Service cost taxpayers $350 million a year, an example of transfer payments from the middle class to the well-to-do.

Children's Television Workshop, producer of the *Sesame Street* children's programs, reaps more than $100 million in licensing fees annually. Its chief executive officer earns $647,000 annually in salary and benefits. A rate card sent out by Washington, D.C., PBS affiliate WETA in 1992 noted that the average net worth of its contributors was $627,000; one in eight was a millionaire; one in seven owned a wine cellar; one in three had been to Europe in the previous three years.

Would privatization cause the death-knell of public broadcasting? Hardly. Private and corporate contributions already make up the vast majority of public broadcasting's revenue. Only 14 percent of the Public Broadcasting Service's (PBS) budget comes from the federal government, and only 3 percent of the National Public Radio's (NPR) budget is composed of federal funds.

Moreover, an eighteen-month experiment allowing advertising on public television in the early 1980s revealed that viewers had no negative reaction to the advertising.[12] In fact, a majority of the respondents supported the concept of advertising on public television.[13]

The sources of information available today have greatly increased over those available in 1967 at the time of the creation of the Corporation for Public Broadcasting. Senator Larry Pressler (R-S. Dak.), Chairman of the Senate Commerce, Science, and Transportation Committee, highlighted some of these new post-1967 sources during his recent testimony before the House Appropriations Committee:

• Broadcast TV stations increased from 769 to 1,688.
• Broadcast radio more than doubled from 5,249 to 11,725.
• The percentage of TV homes subscribing to cable TV grew from 3 percent to 65 percent (cable is available to 96 percent of TV homes).
• CNN, C-SPAN, Arts & Entertainment, Discovery, The Learning Channel, Bravo, The History Channel, and many other cable channels have programming that's a substitute for public broadcasting *without government subsidy.*
• Direct Broadcast Satellite is now available everywhere in the forty-eight contiguous states with over 150 channels of "digital" video and audio programming.
• "Wireless Cable" has several million subscribers.
• More than 85 percent of American homes have a VCR (VCRs were not available in 1967).
• Close to 40 percent of American homes have a per-

113

sonal computer which was not available until the early 1980s.

• Multimedia CD-ROM sales are flourishing with educational titles particularly popular.

• The Internet and computer on-line services such as Prodigy, America OnLine, and Compuserve are reaching more than six million homes.[14]

Even in the area of educational programming, the private sector is using modern technologies to provide access to educational courses in under served and remote areas. For instance, one private company provides access to ten degree programs, as well as credit courses for more than thirty four-year colleges and universities and more than one hundred community colleges through distance learning (using satellite, broadcast, and cable infrastructure).[15]

Furthermore, the privatization of public broadcasting should encourage greater efficiency. According to Senator Pressler, "[a] Twentieth Century Fund study found that 75 cents out of every dollar spent on public broadcasting is spent on overhead." In 1983 an FCC staff study estimated that 40 percent of all public TV stations had signals that overlapped with another public TV station. CPB itself estimates that more than one quarter of the PBS stations are duplicative.[16]

Privatizing the Corporation for Public Broadcasting would also put an end to taxpayer subsidization of works that are offensive to many Americans. The list of such works aired by the Public Broadcasting System or National Public Radio over the years is not insignificant: NPR's recent story focusing on alienated gay men and lesbians fed up with what they think of as the gay mainstream;[17] and, NPR's six-part series featuring a group of eighth-graders explicitly discussing the steps leading up to sexual intercourse.[18]

But the list goes on. PBS has had skirmishes with its audience over the broadcasts of *Tongues of Flame*, an explicit view of homosexuality; *Stop the Church*, a documentary of gay protest in St. Patrick's Cathedral in New York City; and, a point-of-view documentary of a sex change by a man who wished to be a woman.[19]

It is time to eliminate this government subsidization by privatizing the Corporation for Public Broadcasting instead.

Tax-Funded Divorce

Finally, the Legal Services Corporation (LSC) is a federally chartered corporation established to provide legal assistance to the poor. It received an appropriation of $415 million for fiscal year 1995. What many Americans don't realize is that divorce proceedings are a high priority for many legal services grantees.[20] The LSC alone paid for 210,000 divorces in 1990, at an estimated cost to taxpayers of $50 million. Yet, as study after study has revealed, divorce is not helping our nation's poor break out of poverty. Rather, as historian Barbara Dafoe Whitehead has pointed out, "Children in single-parent families are six times as likely to be poor. Twenty-two percent of children in one-parent families will experience poverty during childhood for seven years or more, as compared with only 2 percent of children in two-parent families."[21] Therefore, an agency that was established to help ameliorate poverty is instead fostering it through its financing of divorce actions.

A 1988 report by Kathleen B. DeBettencourt in the Legal Services Corporation's Office of Policy Development raises serious concerns regarding the Legal Services Corporation and its policy on divorce. The report, entitled *Legal Services Corporation vs. The Family*, states in part:

> Since poverty is so often the result of marital dissolution, and since the best means of escaping poverty is through family support, helping families to remain intact must be a priority of any organization working on behalf of the poor.[22]

Notwithstanding, in terms of numbers of cases and resources spent, many legal services grantors give highest priority to divorce proceedings.

Divorce has a deep impact upon women. A woman's income drops an average 73 percent in the first year after divorce; a man's income generally rises. Moreover, in most cases women receive custody of their children; many women, therefore, are responsible for the cost of child care as well as for other expenses. Even if the father is required to contribute to these costs, in many cases the support is minimal. Studies indicate that only 47 percent of women entitled to receive child support actually receive the full amount.

The detrimental impact of divorce is not solely a financial one. Rather, Barbara Dafoe Whitehead has called attention to the fact that "children in single-parent families are two to three times as likely . . . to have emotional and behavioral problems . . . [and] are also more likely to drop out of high school, to get pregnant as teenagers, to abuse drugs, and to be in trouble with the law."[23]

But the Legal Services Corporation's impact on our nation's family policy is not limited to divorce. Rather, the LSC has been very instrumental in shaping our nation's welfare policy. William Mellor, President and General Counsel of the Institute for Justice, recently presented testimony to the United States Senate which detailed the Legal Services Corporation's role in this regard. According to Mellor, "For thirty years Legal Services Corporation-supported organizations have waged a campaign to frustrate any welfare reform that seeks to restrict eligibility for welfare or to limit welfare benefits."[24]

According to Mellor, the LSC pursues an overall welfare litigation strategy involving four goals, the first of which is to establish a right to welfare for all persons in need. In pursuit of this goal, the LSC challenges legislation that excludes classes of individuals, such as college students, as well as challenges eligibility requirements, such as the sources of income used to calculate eligibility for welfare.[25]

The second litigation goal is to prevent welfare eligibility from being dependent upon an agency's whim. Thus, agency eligibility investigations, as well as attempts to restrict welfare based on the behavior of the recipient, have been challenged by LSC-supported attorneys. Mellor pointed out that "[e]very welfare reform plan currently under consideration attempts to link benefits to behavior, but nevertheless LSC funds have been used to challenge restrictions such as work requirements, parental identification, and child support."[26]

The third goal, Mellor explains, is to attack the state and local character of the welfare system. This is "implemented by systematically challenging state laws and attempting to impose federal standards." LSC-sponsored litigators, he notes, have recently challenged state demonstration projects in California, Indiana, Michigan, New Jersey, and Wisconsin. "Advocates receiving LSC funding challenge attempts by states to subject welfare to state budget priorities, or to apportion scarce resources to longer-term residents rather than newcomers."[27]

The fourth and last goal is to secure a right to a certain standard of living through litigation designed to increase benefits, such as challenging the services covered under the welfare or medicaid programs.[28]

Mellor concludes his testimony on the detrimental impact of LSC-sponsored litigation on welfare reform:

[M]ost challenges by LSC-supported attorneys have failed in the courts or eventually been overturned by Congress. But regardless of the success or failure of a particular case, the litigation juggernaut has been relentless. The resulting impact on welfare reform and our social fabric has been highly detrimental. States face the expense and difficulty of defending against aggressively pursued lawsuits when they attempt to reform their laws. New programs undergo years of uncertainty and delay. And a bureaucratic, destructive welfare system threatens to entrap yet another generation.[29]

Christian Coalition urges Congress to privatize all four entities, the NEA, NEH, CPB, and LSC, and turn them into organizations funded through private contributions. To do so would not simply be a matter of fiscal responsibility, it would be a matter of reinstating the proper limits of government.

10

Punishing Criminals, Not Victims

Convicts should be required to work, study, pass random drug testing while in prison, and be required to pay restitution to their victims subsequent to release.

CRIME CAUSES INJURY TO REAL PEOPLE. It can destroy public confidence in the community as a safe place to live and raise a family. Unchecked, it can lead to a disintegration of community values, even a destruction of community dignity. It breeds fear and suspicion. In spite of numerous laws designed to ensure fairly administered justice, today's system is, in plain terms, broken.

Christian Coalition believes that the best reforms we can make right now are reforms that will require of the criminal responsibility, both for the crimes committed and to the victims of those crimes. Such reforms will help restore faith in the judicial system and make the streets safer again for American families and their children.

A Nation of Victims

Crime victims in 1992 lost $17 billion in property theft or damage, cash losses, medical expenses, and amount of pay lost because of injury related to the crime. Every two seconds someone in the United States becomes a victim of crime.[1] Of the thirty-five million crimes committed each year, twenty-five million are serious, involving violence, sizeable loss of property, or both. Each year one in four households is victimized and thirty-six million people are injured as a result of a violent crime.[2]

Moreover, the problem promises to worsen. From 1985 to 1991, homicides committed by boys in the fifteen-to-nineteen-year-old age group increased 154 percent. From 1982 to 1991 the juvenile arrest rate for murder rose 93 percent, for aggravated assault 72 percent, and for forcible rape 24 percent. In the next decade, America will experience a population surge made up of teenage children of today's aging baby boomers. Statistics point to the most violent juvenile crime surge in U.S. history. These children are growing up under appalling family conditions of divorce and illegitimacy. Though repairing the home life where these children are raised is one of the many tasks beyond the reach of government, government can catch and convict lawbreakers—one of its most fundamental roles.

The current debate over crime reform centers around two competing philosophies. Liberals generally argue that crime results from, among other factors, poor education, economic deprivation, racism, and low self-esteem. Their prescription, quite naturally, takes the form of early government intervention with a multitude of programs aimed at job creation and treatment of these external circumstances. Conservatives will generally argue that criminals, not society, are responsible for crime, that crime results from a lack of moral self-restraint, which typically follows from the absence of nurturing parents and their constant discipline. When families fail, government must be ready to deliver a firm message that lawbreaking will not go unpunished and apply an equally firm measure of accountability.[3]

Why Punishment Works

Punishment accomplishes several things. A trial lawyer explained in his book:

First, it emphasizes that we are all part of a community, and it helps define the values that we live by. Certain behavior is wrong, and we expect this to be taught in churches, families, schools, and other institutions in society. When we punish lawbreakers we reinforce these institutions. Second, we say to the offender and to the community that we believe in both freedom of choice and responsibility, and that we will respect freedom by punishing those who violate the law. . . . Third, we say to offenders that we believe they are capable of changing, and that it is important that they choose to change. To do this requires that we treat the individual not as a means to an end, but as someone with innate value, and whose value we want to preserve and enhance. This means that punishment should be a solemn and sad event, not a time for celebration and delight.[4]

Noted criminologist James Q. Wilson lent strength to the argument for swift, sure punishment when he wrote, "There ought to be penalties from the earliest offense . . . so that juveniles are treated by the state the same way we treat our children. You don't ignore the fact that they're wrecking the house until they finally burn it down. You try to deal with it right away."

Criminals Rarely Serve Their Time

The three traditional categories or methods of achieving these ends are deterrence, rehabilitation, and preventing offenders from committing new crimes or incapacitation. While all three have relative merit, they also have been poorly applied and executed in the last thirty years. Today, we have reached a tragic point where nearly three out of every four convicted criminals are not in prison. In fact, by 1990, nearly two-thirds of the more than four million people technically in correctional custody in the U.S. were on probation and 12 percent were on parole.[5] We also have a case where fewer than one in ten serious crimes results in imprisonment.[6]

C. S. Lewis, noted scholar and Christian apologist, wrote, "To be punished, however severely, because we have deserved it, 'because we ought to have known better,' is to be treated as a human person made in the image of God." The current system does not reflect this position in the least. Grounded in the belief that criminals are victims, not victimizers, punishment has been seen as cruel and unusual. Every step in the juvenile court system reflects this orientation toward treatment and rehabilitation and away from accountability and punishment. As one observer from an anticrime advocacy group noted:

> Those who commit crimes while under the age of eighteen are not termed criminals, but are "delinquents." Juveniles are not arrested, they are "taken

into custody." They are not jailed, they are "detained." And they are not charged with a crime, they are "referred" to the court. There, they are not tried; a "hearing" is held. A hearing cannot lead to a conviction and sentencing; it can only lead to a "finding of delinquency" and a "placement" in a "detention center" or "residential facility."

The result of this confusion? The highest juvenile crime rates in American history.

Crime without Punishment

John DiIulio, professor at Princeton University, writes, "There is so much crime without punishment in America today because recent generations of social and political elites, both liberal and conservative, have liberated themselves from the belief that criminals are free moral agents and that publicly sanctioned punishments are what they justly deserve."[7]

Today, 75 percent of inmates are arrested again within four years of their release. Funds dedicated to additional prisons address the reality that even with reform, prisons are routinely overcrowded and there is a need for additional space if violent offenders are to experience the justice of their sentence. In fact, because prison space is such a scarce commodity, when the judge approaches sentencing, many offenders who probably should spend some time away from the public get off with probation or suspended sentences. A well-considered plan that integrates punishment based on a moral principle combined with victim restitution laws is, in fact, the neglected but historically proven method of genuine rehabilitation.

The 1990 census found that "approximately 570,000 inmates, accounting for two-thirds or more of both sexes in state and federal facilities, were not participating in any academic activities." Moreover, about a third of the prison population had no work assignment, and 25 percent was idle—meaning prisoners neither worked nor participated in an academic program.[8]

Payment of Victims

The well-known revolving doors of justice routinely kick-out violent offenders and fill their cells with non-violent check forgers, petty thieves, and tax cheats among others. Restitution can come in many forms, chief of which for many criminals who could not earn more than minimum wage, is work.

Paying a "debt to society" has a proper place and can be filled with appropriate hours of community service. Charles Colson, who went to prison for his part in Watergate, was a lawyer and operated a dryer in the prison laundry room. With him was a skilled doctor who was the former chairman of the board of the American Medical Association. He stirred suds. Both individuals could have paid their societal debts by giving their services free to needy communities. Instead, they were nonviolent offenders taking up prison space and costing taxpayers around $15,000 each plus the $80,000 to build their cells. This process needs to be reexamined.[9]

Education plays an important role in the process of restitution. An estimated 70 percent of inmates are functionally illiterate. One could assume that as these inmates return to society, their chances of holding a decent-paying job are slim. Without reading ability or job skills that could have been practiced and learned in place of pumping iron and watching television, the probability that the offender could then compensate his victim is also quite low. Employing education as one tool in the disciplinary arsenal of correctional facilities would represent one more step toward meeting the rights of victims while not forgetting about the need to try and help the criminal as well.

Criminal Rights Versus Victim Rights

Drug testing for the HIV virus and other diseases would seem like a common sense approach to managing a prison population. Yet "privacy laws" still provide more protection to offenders than to victims and those who work closely with prison populations. Testing for addictive drugs does occur. In 1990, more than 66 percent of men charged with robbery and 68 percent of those charged with burglary tested positive for drugs. Not only is it important to know whether the prison population is at risk from AIDS, there is also a need to know who is on drugs in order to offer drug treatment and a chance to break addictions.

In addition to these measures for those in prisons, change must also make a difference for victims.

When a crime is reported and an arrest is made, the case from then on is referred to as an offense against the state. Cases are titled "People v. the defendant," but common sense tells us that it is more than an offense against the state; it is crime against a human being. Justice, therefore, involves more than just punishing the offender; it also restores the victim. Offenders benefit as well from assuming personal responsibility and performing purposeful work or restitution. Victims may lose life, health, property,

127

or peace of mind and deserve more than only the satisfaction of seeing the perpetrator convicted. Offenders should repay their victims whenever possible. Several barriers, however, stand in the way.

First, most victims have no formal right to receive restitution. Second, even when ordered by a judge, some states lack the resources to enforce the restitution order. Third, many convicted criminals lack good job skills and the financial resources necessary to pay restitution. Probably most obvious, when the state decides to lock up the offender it takes away any ability for the offender to earn money for restitution. Moreover, if a criminal does have financial resources, paying court costs, fees, fines, and other assessments to the court generally takes a higher priority than victim restitution.

The need is staggering. Crime-related injuries typically account for more than 700,000 days of hospitalization annually—the equivalent of about 30 percent of the hospital days for traffic accidents.[10] Property and theft damages are in the billions. Sadly, only 10 percent of theft and burglary victims recover some or all of their stolen property.[11]

Helping Crime Victims

While economic restitution cannot heal emotional trauma, grief, or other personal loss, it does help compensate the victim. And studies show that restitution reduces recidivism, because the criminal becomes aware of the painful consequences of the crime.[12]

Confusion and controversy surround this issue today. Legal experts continue to spar over the interpretation of Congress's intent behind civil forfeiture laws—the seizing of property of convicted offenders, such as bank accounts, boats, and cars. Some courts have ruled that since the offender has already been punished in a criminal case (that is, is now serving prison time), it is "double jeopardy" to take their property in a civil case and is therefore unconstitutional. The question will probably go before the Supreme Court.[13]

Several years ago the *Victim's Rights and Restitution Act* was introduced in Congress and many of its provisions have been enacted into law. In federal court, victims now have the right to be notified of and be involved in court proceedings, the right to be protected from the accused, the right to be treated fairly and with respect, and the right to be informed of the detention status of the convicted criminal. However, even though the *Victim's Rights and Restitution Act* has passed the Senate three times, its restitution provision still has not been enacted into law. Each time it has been dropped in the session where final compromises and details of the bill are worked out. President Clinton's 1994 crime bill followed suit and the restitution provisions were dropped. This provision would have helped ensure that the criminal not only pay his debt to society, but also pay his debt to his victim.

H.R. 665, the *Mandatory Victim Restitution Act of 1995*, passed the House in February and the Senate is concurrently working on a comparable bill. The bill removes all discretionary power of federal judges to decide whether or not to compel restitution. If President Clinton signs the bill, it will be mandatory in all federal cases. Calls to your representative and senators would contribute to the passage of this important law.

Conclusion

THE *CONTRACT WITH THE AMERICAN FAMILY* is the first word, not the last word, on a cultural agenda for the 104th Congress during the post-one-hundred-day period. The ideas included in this document are suggestions, not demands, and are designed to be a help, not a hindrance, to members of Congress as they seek to fulfill their mandate for dramatic change.

Christian Coalition is launching not only the Contract with the American Family, but a nationwide campaign for its enactment. We will spend an estimated $2 million during this session of Congress on newspaper ads, grassroots mailings, phone banks, fax alerts, and radio and television advertising. We will also be mailing between five and ten million households petitions and postcards that they can then return to their members of Congress urging passage of the contract.

Christian Coalition welcomes the support of Republicans and Democrats alike as it seeks passage of the items in this bold legislative agenda. There is no specified deadline on acting on the Contract. The Coalition and its grass-roots members will work on behalf of these mainstream proposals in this Congress and in as many subsequent sessions of Congress as necessary to secure passage.

The American people now have a Congress that is receptive to their desire for religious liberty, stronger families, lower taxes, local control of education, and tougher laws against crime. With the *Contract with the American Family*, the nation now has an agenda with broad support that addresses time-honored values and cultural issues for the 104th Congress and beyond.

Appendix 1

Ralph Reed

Remarks to the Detroit Economic Club
January 17, 1995

"Christian Coalition and an Agenda for the New Congress"

IT IS AN HONOR FOR ME to be with you today in this, one of the nation's most distinguished forums, as we enter the most historic one-hundred-day period in American politics since Franklin Delano Roosevelt swept into office sixty-two years ago.

The American people, the media, and many of you in the business community are still trying to make sense of the new political order ushered in by the 1994 elections. What a different world it is: Speaker Gingrich, Majority Leader Dole, Chairman Archer, and Congressman Sonny Bono. Take heart, Bill Clinton. If Sonny Bono can have a second career in politics, you will be able to have a second career in music. Dan Rostenkowski and Tom Foley are in the unemployment line.

This election has signaled the largest single transfer of power from a majority party to a minority party in the twentieth century. Republicans gained fifty-two house seats, eight Senate seats, eleven governorships, and 472 state legislative seats. In this state, Donald Riegle was replaced by Spence Abraham. In Ohio, Howard Metzenbaum was replaced by Mike DeWine. In Pennsylvania, Harris Wofford was replaced by Rick Santorum. In New York, Mario Cuomo lost in a landslide to George Pataki. These swaps are the political equivalent of Dan Rather handing over the anchor's chair to Rush Limbaugh, or Connie Chung being replaced by Newt Gingrich's mother.

But the election was more than a partisan victory. It was a victory for ideas and ideals. It was a landslide for a particular kind of change: pro-life, pro-family, low tax, and unapologetically committed to restoring traditional values.

It was also, sadly, one of the ugliest campaigns in recent memory. For throughout this last election season, some tried to divide the American people by reference to their religious beliefs. In Massachusetts, a candidate for U.S. Senate was publicly attacked, not because of his stands on the issues, not because of his voting record, but because he was an elder in his church. In South Carolina, a candidate for governor was told that "his only qualifications for office are that he speaks fluently in tongues and handles snakes."

Democratic party officials attacked church-going Americans as "fire-breathing fanatics" and "card-carrying members of the flat earth society." Editorialists warned that Republicans were "in the midst of a blood war for the heart and soul of their party." And "left unchecked, [religious conservatives] could become . . . the secret weapon for Democrats' re-election."

But the exact opposite occurred. They were the key to a conservative tidal wave.

Exit polls found that 33 percent of all voters were self-identified born-again evangelicals or pro-family Roman Catholics. It was the largest turnout of religious voters in modern American political history. They voted 70 percent Republican and only 26 percent Democrat.

It is my fervent hope that these election results will insure that never again will a major political party raise what John F. Kennedy once called "the so-called religion issue." At Christian Coalition, we believe that there should be no religious test, implicit or explicit, to serve in any office of public trust. We believe anyone should be allowed to run for public office without their place of worship becoming an issue. And we believe that church and state should remain separate institutions.

In that spirit, today I issue a challenge to the new chairman of the Democratic National Committee, Senator Chris Dodd of Connecticut. I call on Senator Dodd to repudiate the religious bigotry employed by his party during the last campaign, and to pledge that as national chairman he will not tolerate it in the future. In exchange, we pledge to work with the Democratic Party wherever and whenever possible to advance our mainstream agenda of lower taxes, limited government, tougher laws against crime and drugs, and a restoration of values.

The 1994 elections were also important because they gave people of faith what they have always sought: a place at the table, a sense of legitimacy, and a voice in the conversation that we call democracy. We have become a permanent fixture on the American political landscape, too large, too significant, and too diverse to be ignored by either major political party.

Representative Barney Frank recently rejoiced, "It's

more fun to be in the minority. You don't have to be responsible." Well, Barney, I never thought I would say this, but I hope you have fun for a long time. For us, life is more difficult and the challenge more daunting. We now assume the twin burdens of majority status. First, the requirement of responsibility and reasonableness in governance, both in what we propose and in how we advance it. Second, the burden of seeking what is good for the entire nation, not just our particular constituency. I believe that our shoulders are broad enough, our hearts are big enough, and our spirits are humble enough to carry the responsibility that we now bear.

In the coming months, we must resist the temptation to respond to the attacks that will surely come with the weapons and the words of our critics. We must remain ever cheerful, always positive, calmly confident that the basic decency and fairness of the American people will be with us in the tough days ahead. And we must do more. We must keep our message on the issues—limiting government, reducing taxes, restoring values—and not engage in the character assassination of our foes or the cult of personality among our friends.

We must also, in the words of Martin Luther King, Jr., forsake the violence of the fist, tongue, or heart. For that reason, it has never been more important for us to renounce violence, especially when it originates from within our own ranks. Let me state unequivocally that we condemn the recent terrorism against abortion clinics with all that we are. When demented and deranged individuals take human life in the name of life itself, they are guilty not only of hypocrisy, but of inflicting more harm on our compassionate cause of peace and nonviolence than all our foes put together.

We must also remember, as Bill Clinton forgot, that simply winning an election is not synonymous with victory. Aristotle wrote, "We become brave by doing brave acts." For us, this is a time for boldness. We must be brave enough to be daring, but also mature enough to be patient, always remembering that the wheels of change turn slowly, and the levers of government must be pulled one notch at a time. It took us sixty years to get into this mess, and we will not get out of it overnight.

Ours is a time for compassion, not cruelty; for innovation, not imitation; and for cooperation, not compromise and capitulation. It is a time for hard heads and soft hearts. It is a time, as Abraham Lincoln said, when "The dogmas of the quiet past are inadequate to the stormy present. . . . As our case is new, so we must think anew and act anew."

Lincoln's opponent in the Civil War, Confederate leader Jefferson Davis, was once asked what it would mean if his side lost the war. "You should," he said, "put on our tombstone: *death by a theory*." Well, on November 8, the American public chiseled the epitaph *death by a theory* on the tombstone of liberalism.

Policies once judged by the height of their aspirations are now judged by the depth of their failures—and the magnitude of their casualties—casualties we read about daily in our newspapers and view nightly on our television screens. Our society—any society—cannot survive when its inner cities resemble Beirut, when children pass through metal detectors into schools that are war zones, when one out of every three children is born out of wedlock, and when an African-American male under the age of thirty-five in this city has a higher likelihood of being killed than an American soldier in Vietnam.

Our first step in replacing this tired, liberal order has already begun. For the next eighty-six days, we must simply pass the Contract with America. Christian Coalition will do its part. We will launch the largest single lobbying effort in our history, beginning tomorrow when all fifty of our state chairmen fly to Washington to personally work for passage of the Balanced Budget Amendment. By combining old-fashioned shoe leather politics with the technology of the information highway, we will utilize fax networks, satellite television, computerized bulletin boards, talk radio, and direct mail to mobilize our 1.5 million members and supporters in 1,425 local chapters in support of the Contract. We will spend an estimated $1 million to deluge Capitol Hill with phone calls, faxes, and telegrams. Passing the Contract is critical in restoring the trust and confidence of the American people in their government.

But there is more to be done. What will come after the Contract? Let me suggest four priorities for the new Congress to take up after the first hundred days.

First, the government should promote and defend rather than undermine the institution of the family. As a society, we simply cannot survive another thirty years of no-fault divorce and no-consequence parenthood. The intact family is the most effective department of health, education, and welfare ever conceived. Catholic lay theologian Michael Novak is right when he concludes, "If [the family] fails to teach honesty, courage, desire for excellence and a host of basic skills, it is exceedingly difficult for any other agency to make up for its failures." Our primary task, therefore, is to take power and money away from government bureaucrats in Washington and return it to parents, children, and family.

To this end, we must relieve the crushing tax burden on the American family. The average family of four now spends 38 percent of its income on taxes—more than it spends on food, clothing, housing, and recreation combined. To their credit, the Republicans have proposed a $500 tax credit per child for middle-class working families. That is a good downpayment. But we should go further by tripling or quadrupling the standard deduction for children so that no family of four in America making less than $30,000 pays a dime in federal income tax.

The federal government must no longer subsidize those agencies and programs that promote values contrary to those we teach in our homes. Taxpayer funding for the National Endowment for the Arts, the National Endowment for the Humanities, and the Corporation for Public Broadcasting should be terminated. If we are going to ask single mothers in our inner cities to sacrifice by getting out of the wagon and helping pull it, it is only fair that we require sacrifices from all Americans.

We should also eliminate taxpayer subsidies that encourage family breakups and the taking of innocent human life. According to the Gallup Organization, 72 percent of the American people are opposed to using tax dollars to pay for abortion. We support tightening the Hyde Amendment and ending federal subsidies that threaten human life. In addition, funding for the Legal Services Corporation, which every year pays for 200,000 divorces, should be reduced.

I recently met with the pastor of an African-American church in one of the nation's largest cities who told me that his church sponsors ministry outreach centers to poor minority teens who are at risk for falling into a life of crime or drugs. He went into one such center and asked twelve boys, all under the age of fifteen, how many of them had a father. Not a single boy raised his hand. It is tragic enough that one of every two marriages ends in divorce, and that millions of children in our nation have never known a father, may not know anyone who has a father. It is unconscionable for the federal government to pay for family breakups with tax dollars.

Our goal is not to legislate family values, but to see to it that Washington values families. The values of faith and family that we advance are cherished in our hearts, taught in our schools, honored in our homes, and celebrated in our churches and synagogues. They are not so weak or insecure that they require the agency of the government to win their converts. But it is not too much to ask the government to be the friend rather than the foe of families.

Our second priority is to radically downsize and re-limit government. The values that we espouse are learned, not mandated. These are the values taught around kitchen tables, fathers' knees, during bedtime stories, and at prayer meetings, midnight mass, and Sabbath services. They are values which suffer when weighed down by the heavy hand of government. We subscribe to the old-fashioned wisdom that in a conservative society, traditionalist ends can be achieved through libertarian means. Anything that reduces the role of government bureaucracy and regulations out of our lives and homes is a step in the right direction.

Ronald Reagan once said, "The closest thing to eternal life on earth is a federal program." Well for some of these programs, the time has come for a decent burial. A good first step would be to eliminate several Cabinet departments, including Commerce, Energy, Housing and Urban Development, and Education. In my view, education will be the number one social issue for the remainder of this decade, and our top legislative priority at Christian Coalition is to abolish the Department of Education or downgrade it to agency level. We should defederalize education policy, other than civil rights enforcement, and return it to states, locally elected school boards, and parents. We should return much of the $33 billion we spend at the federal level—70 percent of which never reaches the classroom—and convert it into scholarships or vouchers so that parents can send their children to the best school in their community, whether private, public, or parochial.

Our third priority is to replace the failed and discredited welfare state with a community- and charity-based opportunity society. For most of our history, welfare was the function not of government, but of homes, churches, synagogues, and civic associations like the Salvation Army. This compassionate society was defined by generosity, not by handouts and pity. In this light, the Great Society was not a bold new step, but a failed experiment in social engineering on a massive scale.

Glenn Loury, a brilliant economist from Boston University who also happens to have grown up in the inner city, said recently, "[I]n every community there are agencies of moral and cultural development that seek to shape the ways in which individuals conceive of their duties to themselves, of their obligations to each other, and of their responsibilities before God. . . . If these institutions are not restored, through the devoted agency of the people and not their government, [it] threatens the survival of our republic." We must replace the pity of bureaucrats with the generosity of churches and synagogues; the destructiveness of handouts with the transforming power of responsibility; and, the centralized approach of the Great Society with the care of responsive communities and local government.

The federal government spends nearly $200 billion on 436 welfare programs spread out over four Cabinet departments. The current system penalizes work, discourages marriage, punishes the family, and consigns millions to hopeless poverty. It has enslaved the very people it promised to protect. We recommend consolidating most federal welfare programs into block grants and returning them to the states with a few common-sense strings attached. Reforms that discourage out-of-wedlock births and encourage work. Reforms that allow private institutions to provide help to mothers and children in need. Reforms that reinvigorate rather than atrophy communities. This block grant scheme should not, however, become just another massive new entitlement. The clear goal should be to eliminate, in the course of the next decade, federal involvement in welfare and shift responsibility to private charities and the faith community.

The fourth and final priority of the new Congress should be to secure religious liberty and freedom of conscience for all of our citizens. Too often, a strange hostility and scowling intolerance greets those who bring their private faith into the public square. In Missouri, for example, a child caught praying silently over lunch was sent to week-long detention. In southern Illinois, a fifteen-year-old girl was handcuffed, threatened with mace, and shoved into the back of a police car. Her crime? Praying around the flagpole before school hours. And in Texas, a student drew a picture of his church and his family, only to have it torn up by the teacher.

We believe, as the Supreme Court ruled in *Tinker v. Des Moines School District* in 1969, that a child does not shed his right to freedom of speech when he crosses the schoolhouse gate. Earlier this year, our organization honored Bishop Knox, the African-American principal from Winfield High School in Jackson, Mississippi, who was fired for allowing his students to voluntarily pray. After his dismissal, more than four thousand people gathered at the state capitol in protest. Thirty years ago, people marched on ballot boxes and state capitols in the old confederacy to demand the right to vote. Today, they march on those same state capitols demanding freedom of speech, including speech with a religious content. We are colaborers in that struggle, and we will not rest until their rights are secured.

For us the issue is much broader than voluntary school prayer. We seek to redress three decades of systematic hostility toward religious expression by government agencies, the schools, and the courts. We will propose a religious liberty statute and constitutional amendment, modeled after the *Religious Freedom Restoration Act* of 1993, to guarantee the right of all Americans to express their faith without fear of discrimination or persecution.

These four priorities—ensuring that government is the

friend rather than the foe of the family, limiting government, replacing the welfare state, and securing religious freedom for all—are the embodiment of our legislative agenda. But in the end—and this is important—we will be judged as a movement not by how many precincts we organize, nor how many bills we pass into law, nor how many people are elected to office. We will be judged by how we act and by who we are. As Ralph Waldo Emerson said, "What we are speaks louder than what we say."

As he began his campaign for the presidency in 1860, Abraham Lincoln addressed the students at Cooper Institute. In that speech, he urged that "all parts of this [country] shall be at peace, and in harmony with one another. Let us . . . do our part to have it so. Even though provoked, let us do nothing through passion or ill temper."

Think about the time in which Lincoln uttered those words. Brother prepared to face brother across dark and bloody battlefields, the Union was being torn asunder, and the survival of our form of government hung in the balance. Yet Lincoln's call was for civility and respect for foes. As we begin our crusade, may these words be more than an exhortation. They must be our own Contract with ourselves, our fellow citizens, and with God, as to how we are to carry out our mission. If Lincoln's challenge becomes our challenge, and if his motto becomes our motto, then we can restore America to greatness again.

This past weekend, the Library of Congress put the original hand-written copy of the Gettysburg Address on display for public view. It was the first time that document had been displayed in twenty-two years. How refreshing in an age of cynicism and distrust of government to see thousands of people wait in line for hours to see Lincoln's eloquent words, spoken on the bloodiest battlefield during one of the darkest moments in the worst military conflagration in our nation's history.

All of these changes that we have witnessed in the past few months seemed as unlikely as the uncertain future that lies ahead of us. But there is a force of faith in our public life that cannot be ignored. This faith is the calm assurance that in the end, the truth, no matter how softly spoken and no matter how graciously advanced, will always triumph. So let us begin the important work that lies ahead.

Appendix 2
Additional Sources of Information on Pro-Family Issues

American Family Association
227 Massachusetts Avenue, NE,
  Suite 100A
Washington, D.C. 20002
202/544-0061

Concerned Women for America
370 L'Enfant Promenade, SW,
  Suite 800
Washington, D.C. 20024
202/488-7000

Eagle Forum
316 Pennsylvania Avenue, SE,
  Suite 203
Washington, D.C., 20003
202/544-0353

Family Research Council
700 Thirteenth Street, NW,
  Suite 500
Washington, D.C. 20005
202/393-2100

Focus on the Family
8605 Explorer Drive
Colorado Springs, CO 80920
719/531-3400

Free Congress Foundation
717 Second Street, NE
Washington, D.C. 20002
202/546-3000

Heritage Foundation
214 Massachusetts Avenue, NE
Washington, D.C. 20002
202/546-4400

Home School Legal Defense
  Association
P. O. Box 159
Paeonian Springs, VA 22129
703/338-5600

National Right to Life
419 Seventh Street, NW
Washington, D.C. 20004
202/626-8800

Traditional Values Coalition
139 C Street, SE
Washington, D.C. 20003
202/547-8570

Appendix 3
How to Join with Christian Coalition

Christian Coalition:

- represents Christians before legislative bodies
- speaks out in the public arena and in the media
- trains Christians to be effective leaders
- informs Christians about issues and legislation
- protests anti-Christian bigotry

Christian Coalition State Offices

Christian Coalition of Alabama
2700 Abingdon Road
Birmingham, AL 35243

Christian Coalition of Alaska
P. O. Box 241564
Anchorage, AK 99524

Christian Coalition of Arizona
P. O. Box 16994
Phoenix, AZ 85011

Christian Coalition of Arkansas
P. O. Box 2083
Jonesboro, AR 72401

Christian Coalition of California
14039 Sherman Way,
   Suite 202
Van Nuys, CA 91405

Christian Coalition of Colorado
1100 W. Littleton Boulevard,
   Suite 203
Littleton, CO 80120

Christian Coalition of
   Connecticut
P. O. Box 372
Quinebaug, CT 06262

Christian Coalition of Delaware
18 Fox Hunt Drive
Bear, DE 19701

Christian Coalition of Florida
P. O. Box 560219
Orlando, FL 32856

Christian Coalition of Georgia
3937 Holcomb Bridge Road
Suite 300
Norcross, GA 30092

Christian Coalition of Hawaii
1132 Kaumarluna Place
Honolulu, HI 96817

Christian Coalition of Idaho
P. O. Box 581
Boise, ID 83701

Christian Coalition of Illinois
P. O. Box 1776
Bloomington, IL 61702

Christian Coalition of Indiana
7802 Cannonade Drive
Indianapolis, IN 46217

Christian Coalition of Iowa
3375 X. Avenue
West Des Moines, IA 50266

Christian Coalition of Kansas
13223 W. 107th Court
Lenexa, KS 66210

Christian Coalition of Kentucky
3346 Bluejay Drive
Edgewood, KY 41018

Christian Coalition of Louisiana
306 Legendre Drive
Slidell, LA 70460

Christian Coalition of Maine
260 Ludlow Street
Portland, ME 04102

Christian Coalition of Maryland
10101 Hummingbird Street
Ellerslie, MD 21529

Christian Coalition of
  Massachusetts
4 Glenbrook Lane
Worcester, MA 01609

Christian Coalition of Michigan
401 S. Woodward Avenue,
  Suite 317
Birmingham, MI 48009

Christian Coalition of Minnesota
2675 Patton Road
Saint Paul, MN 55113

Christian Coalition of
  Mississippi
161 Pole Bride Road
Brandon, MS 39042

Christian Coalition of Missouri
9409 E. 63rd Street
Raytown, MO 64133

Christian Coalition of Montana
921 Euclid Avenue
Helena, MT 59601

Christian Coalition of Nebraska
P. O. Box 3801
Omaha, NE 68103

Christian Coalition of Nevada
1975 Ives Avenue
Reno, NV 89503

Christian Coalition of New
  Hampshire
67 Emerald Street, Suite 423
Keene, NH 03431

Christian Coalition of New
  Jersey
RD #7, Box 158D
Woodruff Road
Bridgeton, NJ 08302

Christian Coalition of New
  Mexico
8509 La Palomita Road, NE
Albuquerque, NM 87111

Christian Coalition of New York
P. O. Box 432
Clarence, NY 14031

Christian Coalition of North
  Carolina
P. O. Box 591
Lexington, NC 27292

Christian Coalition of North
  Dakota
RR2, Box 77
Northwood, ND 78267

Christian Coalition of Ohio
7557 Kittery Lane
Mentor, OH 44060

Christian Coalition of Oklahoma
P. O. Box 2460
Norman, OK 73070

Christian Coalition of Oregon
15790 S. Lammer Road
Oregon City, OR 97045

Christian Coalition of
  Pennsylvania
900 Samoset
Harrisburg, PA 17109

Christian Coalition of Rhode
  Island
P. O. Box 602
Davisville, RI 02854

Christian Coalition of South
  Carolina
8740 Northpark Boulevard,
  Suite 300
Charleston, SC 29406

Christian Coalition of South
  Dakota
P. O. Box 1580
Rapid City, SD 57709

Christian Coalition of Tennessee
1621 E. Magnolia Avenue,
  Suite C
Knoxville, TN 37917

Christian Coalition of Texas
1600 Airport Freeway, Suite 506
Bedford, TX 76022

Christian Coalition of Vermont
P. O. Box 581
Barre, VT 05641

Christian Coalition of Virginia
P. O. Box 6754
Richmond, VA 23230

Christian Coalition of
  Washington
3430 Pacific Avenue, SE,
  Suite A6-336
Olympia, WA 98501

Christian Coalition of Wisconsin
P. O. Box 4061
Waukesha, WI 53187

Christian Coalition of Wyoming
2232 Dell Range Boulevard,
  Suite 310
Cheyenne, WY 82009

Notes

Chapter 1

1. Keith A. Fournier, *Religious Cleansing in the American Republic*, 1993, 16.
2. Catholic League for Religious and Civil Rights, Catholic League's 1994 Report on Anti-Catholicism, 14.
3. Ibid.
4. Fournier, 16.
5. Only after the student's parent contacted the school board was the book allowed.
6. Mark Kellner, "Postal Grinch Who Stole Christmas," *The Washington Times*, November 20, 1994; Catholic League for Religious and Civil Rights, 1994 Report, 17.
7. Catholic League, 1994 Report, 16.
8. David Barton, *The Myth of Separation*, WallBuilder Press, 1992.
9. Jesse H. Choper, *The Establishment Clause and Aid to Parochial Schools—An Update*, 75 Cal. L. Rev., 5, 6–7, 1987.
10. Nationwide survey conducted by Luntz Research and Strategic Services, August 1994. Sample size: 1,200; theoretical margin of sampling error: + or −3%.

Chapter 2

1. William J. Bennett, *The Index of Leading Cultural Indicators*, The Heritage Foundation, March 1993, 17.
2. Claudia Wallis, "A Class of Their Own," *Time*, October 31, 1994, 56.
3. Maria Koklanaris, "Virginia Parents May Get Option to Exclude Pupils from Counseling." *The Washington Times*, October 28, 1994.
4. Lynne V. Cheney, "The End of History," *The Wall Street Journal*, October 20, 1994.
5. Ibid.

6. Ibid.
7. See *Congressional Record*, January 18, 1995, S1025-2040.
8. Claudia Wallis, "A Class of Their Own," 56.

Chapter 3

1. National Committee on Excellence in Education, *A Nation At Risk*, 1983.
2. David R. Henderson, *The Case for School Choice*, Hoover Institute Press, 1993.
3. *Report Card on American Education 1993*, Empower America and the American Legislative Exchange Council, September 1993.
4. U.S. Department of Education, Center for Choice in Education, Issue Brief (Executive Summary), "Public Opinion on Choice in Education," March 1992.
5. The Heritage Foundation, "School Choice Continues to Gain Ground," *Business/Education Insider*, June/July, 1994.
6. Harold Johnson, "The 174 Fight," *National Review*, October 1, 1993.
7. Bret Schundler, "The Simple Logic of School Choice," *The New York Times*, October 28, 1993.
8. Quoted in K. L. Billingsley, "School Daze in California," *Heterodoxy*, September 1993, 4.
9. Allyson M. Tucker, "The Carnegie Foundation's Shabby Assault on School Choice," *Heritage Foundation Backgrounder*, May 10, 1993.
10. National Governors Association, *Time for Results: The Governors 1991 Report on Education*, 1986.

Chapter 4

1. 262 U.S. 390 (1923)
2. Ibid., 399
3. 268 U.S. 510 (1925)
4. Ibid., 518
5. *Brown v. Hot, Sexy and Safer Productions, Inc.*, CN 93-CV-11842K (D.Mass. filed Dec. 1993).
6. *Gardini v. Moyer*, 575 N.E.2d 423 (Ohio 1991).
7. Ibid., 425

8. *In re* Sumey, 94 Wash.2d 757, 621 P.2d 108 (1980).
9. Ibid.
10. *In re* Sampson, 65 Misc.2d 658, 317 N.Y.S.2d 641 (Fam.Ct. 1970), aff'd. 377 App. Div.2d 668, 323 N.Y.S.2d 253 (1971), aff'd. 29 N.Y.S.2d 900, 278 N.E.2d 918, 328 N.Y.S.2d 686 (1972).
11. "Whose Child Is This?" *The New American*, November 28, 1994, 23.
12. Cynthia Price Cohen and Howard Davison, *Children's Rights in America*: UN Convention on the Rights of The Child *Compared with United States Law*, American Bar Association, 1990.
13. Ibid., 177.
14. Ibid., 182.
15. Ibid., 180.
16. Ibid., 182.
17. Ibid.

Chapter 5

1. Robert Rector, *Heritage Backgrounder*, The Heritage Foundation, March 7, 1994.
2. House Republican Conference Talking Points, *May 6: Freedom From Taxes*, May 3, 1995.
3. Allison L. Cowan, "Women's Gains on the Job: Not Without a Heavy Toll," *The New York Times*, October 21, 1989.
4. William R. Mattox, Jr., "The Parent Trap," *Policy Review*, Winter 1991.
5. Rector (based on income data from the U.S. Bureau of the Census).
6. Allan Carlson, *Taxation and the Family: Philosophical and Historical Considerations*, Family Research Council, February 1994.
7. House Republican Conference Talking Points.
8. Rob Norton, "Our Screwed-Up Tax Code," *Fortune*, September 6, 1993.
9. "Clinton's New Taxes," *The Wall Street Journal*, June 25, 1993.
10. Robert J. Barro, "Higher Taxes, Lower Revenues," *The Wall Street Journal*, July 9, 1993.

Chapter 6

1. Mother Teresa of Calcutta, remarks at the National Prayer Breakfast, February 3, 1994.

2. John T. Noonan, Jr., "An Almost Absolute Value in History," in *The Morality of Abortion,* Harvard University Press, 1970.

3,4. Barbara J. Syska, Thomas W. Hilgers, M.D., and Dennis O'Hare, "An Objective Model for Estimating Criminal Abortions and Its Implications for Public Policy," *New Perspectives on Human Abortion,* University Publications of America, 1981. The authors took the figures for legal abortions for 1969–72 from Centers for Disease Control reports. The authors concluded, "It is not true that legal abortion simply replaces criminal abortion. With legalized abortion, there is an exponential increase in the *total* number of abortions each year in the United States, in the range of six- to eleven-fold from the prelegalization era [i.e., prior to 1967]."

5. Figures for legal abortions after *Roe v. Wade* taken from "Abortion Services in the United States," Alan Guttmacher Institute, *Family Planning Perspectives,* March/April 1987.

6. Diane M. Gianelli, "Abortion Providers Share Inner Conflicts," *American Medical News,* July 12, 1993.

7. Gracie S. Hsu, "Suffer the Children: Title X's Family Planning Failure," Family Research Council, 1995.

8. Transcript of White House press briefing, April 1, 1993.

9. "Statement of the Honorable Timothy E. Wirth, U.S. Representative to the Second Preparatory Committee for the International Conference on Population and Development," U.S. Mission to the United Nations, May 11, 1993, 5.

10. State Department cable "to all diplomatic and consular posts," March 16, 1994.

11. Nafis Sadik, executive director, United Nations Population Fund, "Safeguarding the Future," remarks to Capitol Hill briefing, May 24, 1989 (audio recording), and interview on *CBS Nightwatch,* November 21, 1989.

12. In a ruling written by Judge Abdner Mikva, a three-judge panel of the U.S. Court of Appeals for the District of Columbia ruled unanimously that a sworn statement from the administrator of the

federal Agency for International Development (AID) "of how the UNFPA's activities in China aid the [coercive] aspects of China's program that Congress condemned amply supports his conclusion that funding UNFPA is prohibited by the [Kemp] amendment." [*Population Institute v. McPherson*, Civil Action No. 85-6042, August 12, 1986, 23.]

13. Amnesty International USA statement, "People's Republic of China: Catholic Villagers in Hebei Province," March 14, 1995.
14. Transcript, briefing by Undersecretary of State for Global Affairs Tim Wirth, April 24, 1995.
15. Report issued by the Gallup Organization on CNN/*USA Today*/ Gallup Poll, February 24–26, 1995.
16. The Gallup Organization, "Abortion and Moral Beliefs," based on a survey of 2,100 adult Americans, released February 28, 1991.
17. Figures from the Alan Guttmacher Institute, cited by Diane M. Gianelli, "Shock-Tactic Ads Target Late-Term Abortion Procedure," *American Medical News*, July 5, 1993.
18. C. Everett Koop, M.D., Surgeon General of the United States, letter to the Honorable Christopher H. Smith, February 24, 1984.
19. Diane M. Gianelli, "Shock-Tactic Ads Target Late-Term Abortion Procedure," *American Medical News*, July 5, 1993.
20. Liz Jeffries and Rick Edmonds, "The Dreaded Complication," *Philadelphia Inquirer*, August 2, 1981.
21. Gianna Jessen, who survived an attempted abortion in 1977, tells her story in *Gianna: Aborted . . . And Lived to Tell About It*, by Jessica Shaver: Focus on the Family Publishing, 1995.
22. Warren H. Hern, M.D., M.P.H., "What About Us? Staff Reactions to the D & E Procedure," paper presented to the Association of Planned Parenthood Physicians, San Diego, October 26, 1978, 7–8.
23. David Daley, "Late Abortion Pushes Medicine to Edge," *Dayton Daily News*, December 10, 1989.
24. Paul J. Rinalli, M.D., "Troubling Thoughts About the Pain of Abortion to Unborn Babies," *National Right to Life News*, May 17, 1995.
25. Diane M. Gianelli, "Shock-Tactic Ads Target Late-Term Abortion Procedure."

26. Ibid.
27. Martin Haskell, M.D., "Dilation and Extraction for Late Second Trimester Abortion," paper presented at the National Abortion Federation Risk Management Seminar, September 13, 1992.
28. Diane M. Gianelli, "Shock-Tactic Ads Target Late-Term Abortion Procedure."
29. Barbara Radford, executive director, National Abortion Federation, letter to federation members, June 18, 1993.
30. The nonpartisan Congressional Budget Office estimated that if the Hyde Amendment and other similar restrictions on federal funding of abortion were removed, "the federal government would probably fund between 325,000 to 675,000 abortions each year." Letter from CBO Director Robert D. Reischauer to Congressman Vic Fazio, July 19, 1993.
31. Governor Bill Clinton, letter to Arkansas Right to Life, September 26, 1986.
32. Transcript of White House press briefing, March 2, 1995.

Chapter 7

1. National Center for Policy Analysis, "Why Not Abolish the Welfare State?" *Executive Summary*, October 1994.
2. Ibid.
3. Marvin Olasky, "Dependent No More," *Christianity Today*, August 17, 1992, 30–33.
4. National Center for Policy Analysis, "Why Not Abolish the Welfare State?"

Chapter 8

1. "Sex on the Info Highway," *Newsweek*, March 14, 1994, 62.
2. John Zipperer, "The Naked City," *Christianity Today*, September 12, 1994, 42.
3. Stephen Bates, "The First Amendment in Cyberspace," *The Wall Street Journal*, June 1, 1994.
4. Phil Long, "Computer Cop Keeping Superhighway Clean," *Miami Herald*, July 14, 1994.
5. Quoted in John Zipperer, "The Naked City," 42.

6. "Right Answer Sex, Wrong Answer Slap," *Newsweek*, March 14, 1994, 62–63.
7. Amy Harmon, "The 'Seedy' Side of CD-ROMs," *The Los Angeles Times*, November 29, 1993.

Chapter 9

1. Robert Pear, "Arts Endowment will be Battling for Existence," *The New York Times*, January 9, 1995.
2. Written Testimony of William J. Bennett before the Subcommittee on Interior of the House Committee on Appropriations, 104th Congress, First Session, January 24, 1995.
3. Rod Dreher, "S&M 'Art' Video Exceeds Shocking Stage Version," *The Washington Times*, January 26, 1995.
4. *Bella Lewitzky Dance Foundation v. Frohmayer*, 754 F. Supp. 774 (C.D. Cal. 1991).
5. *Finley v. National Endowment for the Arts*, 795 F. Supp. 1457 (C.C. Cal. 1992).
6. Robert H. Knight, "The National Endowment for the Arts: Misusing Taxpayers' Money," Heritage Foundation *Backgrounder* No. 803, January 18, 1991, 28.
7. Ibid., 27.
8. Written Testimony of Lynne V. Cheney before the Subcommittee on Interior of the House Committee on Appropriations, 1.
9. Written Testimony of William J. Bennett before the Subcommittee on Interior of the House Committee on Appropriations, 5.
10. Written Testimony of Lynne V. Cheney before the Subcommittee on Interior of the House Committee on Appropriations, 2.
11. Written Testimony of William J. Bennett before the Subcommittee on Interior of the House Committee on Appropriations, 4.
12. Written Testimony of William J. Bennett before the Subcommittee on Interior of the House Committee on Appropriations, 6.
13. Written Testimony of Senator Larry Pressler, Chairman, Commerce, Science and Transportation Committee, United States Senate before the House Committee on Appropriations, 104th Congress, First Session, January 19, 1995, 4–5.
14. Ibid.
15. Written Testimony of Dr. Bernard Luskin, President, Jones Edu-

cation Networks, before the Subcommittee On Labor, Health and Human Services, Education, and Related Agencies of the House Committee on Appropriations, 104th Congress, First Session, January 19, 1995, 4.

16. Written Testimony of Senator Larry Pressler before the House Committee on Appropriations, 2–3.

17. Written Testimony of Senator Larry Pressler before the House Committee on Appropriations, 104th Congress, First Session, January 19, 1995, 2.

18. Thomas B. Edsall, " 'Defunding' Public Broadcasting: Conservative Goal Gains Audience," *The Washington Post*, April 15, 1995.

19. Marilyn Duff, "PBS Flaunts Promiscuous Gays of '70s San Francisco," *Human Events*, February 18, 1994.

20. Kathleen B. DeBettencourt, Office of Policy Development, Legal Services Corporation, *Legal Services Corporation vs. the Family*, March 1988, 15.

21. Barbara Dafoe Whitehead, "Dan Quayle Was Right," *Atlantic Monthly*, April 1993, 47.

22. Kathleen B. DeBettencourt, *Legal Services Corporation v. the Family*, 15.

23. Barbara Dafoe Whitehead, "Dan Quayle Was Right," 47.

24. Written Testimony of William Mellor, President and General Counsel, Institute for Justice Before the Subcommittee on Commerce, State, and Justice of the Senate Committee on Appropriations, 104th Congress, First Session, May 17, 1995, 1.

25. Ibid., 5.

26. Ibid., 5–6.

27. Ibid., 6.

28. Ibid., 6.

29. Ibid., 7–8.

Chapter 10

1. Patsy J. Klaus, *The Costs of Crime to Victims*, U.S. Department of Justice, February 1994. NCJ-145865.

2. Bureau of Justice Statistics, *Highlights from Twenty Years of Surveying Crime Victims*, U.S. Department of Justice, October 1993. NCJ-144525.

Notes

3. Paul J. McNulty, "Natural Born Killers?" *Policy Review*, Winter 1995, 84–87.

4. Daniel W. Van Ness, *Crime and Its Victims*, Intervarsity Press, 1986, 87–88.

5. U.S. Department of Justice, Bureau of Justice Statistics, cited in John J. DiIulio, Jr., "The Value of Prisons," *The Wall Street Journal,* May 13, 1992.

6. Ibid.

7. John J. DiIulio, "The Crime of Not Punishing, A History of U.S. Justice," *The Washington Times*, September 12, 1993.

8. U.S. Department of Justice, Bureau of Justice Statistics, "Census of State and Federal Correctional Facilities, 1990." A survey of state prison inmates in 1991 also substantiated that approximately one-third of the inmates had no work assignments. See Bureau of Justice Statistics, "Survey of State Prison Inmates, 1991."

9. Charles Colson, and Daniel Van Ness, *Convicted: New Hope for Ending America's Crime Crisis,* Crossway Books, 1989, 9.

10. H.R. Rep. No. 104–16, 104th Congress, First Session, 1995.

11. Bureau of Justice Statistics, *Highlights from Twenty Years of Surveying Crime Victims.* U.S. Dept. of Justice. October 1993. NCJ-144525.

12. Paul J. McNulty, *Natural Born Killers?* 84–87.

13. Ronald J. Ostrow, "U.S. Seeks to Reverse Bar to Seizure of Felons' Assets," *Los Angeles Times*, October 21, 1994.

About Christian Coalition

Christian Coalition is a grass-roots citizen organization founded in 1989 for the purpose of giving people of faith a voice in government. The pro-family group is composed of evangelicals, Roman Catholics, Jews, Greek Orthodox, and other people of faith, and has established itself as one of the largest and most effective civic organizations in America today.

Christian Coalition now has 1.6 million members and supporters in 1,600 local chapters in all fifty states. The Coalition utilizes a vast network of more than 60,000 churches to educate voters about current issues affecting families. Christian Coalition's headquarters is located in Chesapeake, Virginia, with legislative offices in Washington, D.C., as well.

Christian Coalition educates voters in a variety of ways. Prior to the 1994 elections, Christian Coalition distributed more than sixty million pieces of nonpartisan voter education literature that explained where candidates stood on a wide range of issues. The group's nonpartisan voter guides, congressional scorecards, and satellite television broadcasts were widely credited with contributing to a record number of religious conservative voters turning out to the polls.

Christian Coalition plays a vital role in shaping the public policy debate. Through numerous media appearances, testimony before Congress, and media advertising campaigns, Christian Coalition has become a leading representative of pro-family Americans who wish to have a voice in the civic debate.

About Christian Coalition

If you are interested in learning more about Christian Coalition, call toll free 1-800-325-4746, or write to Christian Coalition at 1801-L Sara Drive, Chesapeake, Virginia 23320. Internet users may read the latest information distributed by Christian Coalition by contacting Christian Coalition's World Wide Webb home page at http://www.cc.org.